W.H. Strobridge

Catalogue of a valuable collection of ancient and modern coins and medals, comprising ... the cabinet formed by the late Col. James H. Taylor, ... with selections from others and an addenda :

to be sold at auction by Messrs. Geo. A. Leavitt & Co., at

W.H. Strobridge

Catalogue of a valuable collection of ancient and modern coins and medals, comprising ... the cabinet formed by the late Col. James H. Taylor, ... with selections from others and an addenda :
to be sold at auction by Messrs. Geo. A. Leavitt & Co., at

ISBN/EAN: 9783741182143

Manufactured in Europe, USA, Canada, Australia, Japa

Cover: Foto ©Andreas Hilbeck / pixelio.de

Manufactured and distributed by brebook publishing software (www.brebook.com)

W.H. Strobridge

Catalogue of a valuable collection of ancient and modern coins and medals, comprising ... the cabinet formed by the late Col. James H. Taylor, ... with selections from others and an addenda :

CATALOGUE

OF A

VALUABLE COLLECTION

OF

ANCIENT AND MODERN

Coins and Medals,

COMPRISING

THE WHOLE OF THE CABINET FORMED BY THE

Late Col. JAMES H. TAYLOR, of Charleston, S. C.

WITH SELECTIONS FROM OTHERS, AND AN ADDENDA.

TO BE SOLD AT AUCTION

BY MESSRS. GEO. A. LEAVITT & CO., AT THEIR SALE ROOMS,

Clinton Hall, Astor Place, New York,

ON THE AFTERNOON OF

Tuesday, November 16th,

AND FOLLOWING DAYS UNTIL ALL IS SOLD,

COMMENCING EACH DAY AT 3 O'CLOCK.

The Messrs. LEAVITT, Auctioneers.

CATALOGUED BY WILLIAM H. STROBRIDGE.

1875.

INTRODUCTION.

The collector of coins, whatever his specialty may be, cannot fail to find something in this Catalogue to his taste. The genuine numismatist is interested in every medal or piece of money, of whatever nation or age it may be, remarkable for rarity, extraordinary merit as a work of art, uncommon preservation, or historical importance.

The great *variety* in the Taylor cabinet, while it made it interesting as a collection, may be considered a fortunate characteristic—now that it is to be sold.

Had the writer in view only the interests of those who *sell* these coins, he might endeavor to stimulate competition for particular lots by naming them here, and pointing out the most valuable; but the study of coins has in this community now advanced somewhat beyond the rudiments of numismatic science, and this catalogue will fall into hands, to say the least, as well qualified as himself to make comparisons and draw conclusions; and having given, so far as he was capable, a plain and truthful account of what was confided to his care, he will consider his task completed, after having made a few observations as general as the nature of the subject will permit.

There will always be some difference of opinion concerning the proper description of a coin. In other communities the points discussed have been, and it is to be hoped will continue to be, nearly related to the origin, meaning, and importance of the coin itself; among ourselves, criticism has occupied itself with the extent of the significance of the word *fine*, and more particularly with the vast difference between the meaning of that term when standing alone (like a shield of arms without supporters), or when preceded by the adverb *very*.

Whether the writer is or is not so loyal to the decrees of those who preside in the temples which men in these degenerate days have dedicated to the goddess Moneta as to be of the opinion of Tacitus, "That it is more pious and respectful to believe than to inquire into the works of the gods," he is, at least, too sensible of what is due to popular prejudice to call a coin fine simply because it has high antiquity, admirable art, and important meaning to recommend it, unless it has also that other quality which we expect in the proof-sets of the current year of grace—a brilliant surface, unsoiled by the contact of human hands, or the baser contact of other metals.

Should any one think these remarks inspired by personal or professional promptings, the answer is made—Most decidedly they are not.

There is but one man to whom a *personal* disclaimer is due, and to that man the coin cabinets of America owe more than to any other. He set up his standard on the mountain-tops—perfection was his touchstone. When that was impossible, *the best attainable* was the rule and limitation. Those who come after him will

"Follow in the furrows that he tilled,"

or they will sink out of sight.

To return from what has narrowly escaped being a digression: The ancient coins with which the Catalogue begins are, with a single exception, more considerable in numbers and quality than have appeared in any sale in New York during the last ten years. Among the medals are some that are rare, as well as many that are fine, and the Papal series is unusually full, and contains several of much interest.

In Part II. will be found some of the most valuable coins that are known to our national history, both before and after the establishment of the Mint.

No. 548 is a medal concerning which the writer hopes to receive some information before the sale takes place, and invites any one to kindly communicate their views on this or any other subject connected with the Catalogue. W. H. STROBRIDGE.

CLINTON HALL, Oct. 18th, 1875.

TABLE OF CONTENTS.

Antique Greek Coins,	1
The Roman As, with its Divisions,	6
Denarii of Roman Families,	7
Roman Imperial Coins,	14
Jewish Coins,	25
Antique Christian Medals,	25
American Colonial Coins,	26
Coins of the United States Mint,	27
American Medals,	36
Presidential,	39
Army,	40
Navy,	41
Anglo-Saxon and English,	43
English Copper Coins and Tokens,	49
Coins and Medals of France,	50
Silver Coins of Spain and Mexico,	52
Coins of Portugal and Brazil,	53
Coins of Italy,	55
Coins of Denmark, Norway and Sweden,	57
Miscellaneous Foreign Coins,	57
Oriental Coins,	58
Papal Medals and Coins,	59
Bronze Medals,	63

Part II.

Colonial and State Coins and Tokens,	65
United States Coins, from the establishment of the Mint,	68
American Medals,	92
Commemorative Medals and Tokens,	97
Store Cards,	98
English Silver Coins,	99
English Copper Coins,	100

Table of Contents.

English Colonies and Trade Tokens, . . . 101
English Medals, ... 102
Silver Coins of France, ... 103
Copper Coins and Medals of France, . . 103
Spain and Mexico, ... 105
Portugal and Brazil, ... 105
Central and South American Republics and West Indies, ... 106
Oriental Coins, with Turkey and Greece, . . 106
Coins of Russia, ... 107
Coins of Sweden, ... 108
Coins of Italy, ... 108
Miscellaneous Silver Coins, ... 109

ADDENDA.

Colonial and State Coins, ... 110
Cents, ... 110
Half-Cents, ... 112
Dollars, ... 112
Half-Dollars, ... 112
Quarter-Dollars, ... 113
Dimes, ... 114
Half-Dimes, ... 114
Three Cents, ... 115
Electrotypes, ... 115
American Medals and Tokens, ... 115
Foreign Silver Coins, ... 116
Copper Medals, Coins, and Tokens, . . . 116
Ancient Coins, ... 117
American Silver Coins, etc., ... 117
Numismatic Books, ... 119
English Catalogues, (bound), ... 120
Priced Catalogues, (American Sales), . . . 121
Miscellaneous, ... 122

CATALOGUE.

ANTIQUE COINS.

Greek.

1 AEGINA (island of Attica); Tortoise in high relief; rev. punch mark in 4 equal spaces; in fine preservation; r. di. S.
2 —— Same, with counter-mark, (Greek S.) on back of tortoise; rev. 5 irregular punch marks. Equally fine.
3 AGRIGENTUM (Sicily); Eagle standing; AKRA; rev. in hollow, crab. Fine, r. di. S.
4 —— Head of Apollo, rev. two eagles tearing a hare; same, rev. Eagle standing; to l. crab; and other reverses; various sizes, C. 5 p
5 AGATHOCLES (tyrant, Sicily); head of Diana to r. SOT EIRA; rev. winged thunderbolt; C. Uncommonly fine; and one of Antioch. Size 15; 2 p
6 ANTIOCHUS 8th, (Grypus, King of Syria); head diademed; rev. Jupiter seated holding victory and hasta, a crown of laurel surrounding; as fine as when struck. Very rare; Tet. S.
7 ALEXANDER (Magnus, King of Macedon); head, with lion's scalp; rev. Jupiter seated; with his title as king in ex. Extremely fine; Tet. S. Size 16
8 —— Another pierced; also drachm. 2 p

Antique Coins.

9 ATHENS (Attica); head of Minerva; rev. Owl; to l. spray of olive; clump form. Ex. fine; Tet. S.
            Size 14 x 15
10 —— Same. Very fine.   Size 12 x 14
11 —— Another. Good.   " 14 x 16
12 —— Drachm, and two copper coins.   3 p
13 BRUTTIUM (Italy); head of Jupiter laureated, and head helmeted; rev. on both armed figure charging to r. Patinated and fine; C.   Size 16 and 14; 2 p
14 —— Winged head of Victory; rev. Bacchus standing; fine work, in fair preservation; di. S.
15 CALES (Campania); head of Pallas; rev. Victory in a biga; CALENO; S. di.; fair; (rare).
16 CAULONIA (in Bruttium); Stag to r.; rev. Figure nearly nude striking to r.; S. di.; fair; two varieties.
17 —— Drachma; same type, and another pierced. 2
18 CORINTH (Achiæ); head of Pallas to l.; in the field lance; rev. Pegassus; below, A. Extremely fine an broad; di. S.
19 —— Same type; behind head of Pallas, crown; and below Pegassus, Phenician Koph. Very fine; di. S.
20 —— Same; with head of Pallas to r., and Pegassus to r which is very unusual. Fine; di. S.
21 —— Same; head to l.; in field Macedonian shield; rev Pegassus to l. Fine di.
22 —— Another; with different symbols. Very fine.
23 —— Others; in fair condition; full size.   6
24 CUMEA (Italy); female head to r.; rev. shell and gra of barley; S. di., large size; well preserved and rare
25 CROTONA (Bruttium); Tripod in relief; rev. same, incuse well preserved; S. di; (rare 5.)
26 —— Tripod; rev. raven; di. Very rare.
27 —— Head of Juno; rev. tripod; di. Very rare.
28 DEMETRIUS I. (Syria); head; rev. female seated, a Titan supporting her seat, in her hands a baton and horn of plenty; Greek legend and various monograms; S. Tet. Very fine and rare.
29 EGYPT; Ptolemy 1st, and Berenice; head of both diademed, hers with hair in long curls; three sizes, C 8 to 16. Rare.   3

Greek.

30 BERENICE, wife of Ptolemy I.; head, with long curls; rev. eagle on thunderbolt, wings raised; C. Fine.
Size 16

31 —— Cleopatra, wife of Ptolemy; head of Cleopatra in elephant's skin hood ; rev. eagle on a thunderbolt. In excellent preservation, and rare ; C. Size 15

32 —— Ptolemy Evergetes; head of Jupiter Ammon diademed ; rev. eagle standing on a thunderbolt; in field a horn of plenty. Fine ; C. Size 22

33 —— Ptolemy VIII. ; same head ; rev. eagles (2) standing on thunderbolt; in field horn of plenty. Well patinated, and very fine ; C. Size 20

34 —— Another; Ptolemy VIII. Fine. Size 26

35 —— Ptolemy IX. (Alexander I.); young head beardless, covered with the elephant's scalp ; rev. eagle on thunderbolt with raised wings. Fine ; C. Size 14 ; 2 p

36 —— Ptolemy VIII. and IX.; C. Size 16 ; 2 p

37 —— Ptolemy (which, is uncertain); head of Jupiter Dodonœus (crowned with oak); rev. eagle on thunderbolt ; in field a cornucopia. *Extremely* fine ; C.
Size 23

38 —— Other large copper coins. 5 p

39 —— (or Carthage). Small C. 6 p

40 HYRIUM (Italy); head of Minerva; owl on helmet; rev. bull with human face to r; name in Greek. Very rare ; di. S.

41 HERACLIA (Lucania); head of Pallas; syren on helmet ; rev. Hercules strangling a lion ; in the field, bow and arrow ; another, with lion walking to l. ; S. di. Good.
2 p

42 LEONTIUM (Sicily) ; head of Ceres ; rev. lion's head, open mouth ; around 4 grains of barley ; LEON TI NON. Well preserved, and rare ; Tet. S.

43 —— Another Tet., slightly different. Equally fine and rare.

44 MAMERTINI (Sicily); helmeted and bearded head ; rev. Victory erecting a trophy, and other varieties ; C. Various sizes. 4 p

Antique Coins.

45 MESSANA (Sicily); hare running to r.; name of the City; rev. biga; in ex. fish. In excellent preservation. S. Tet. · Size 17
46 METAPONTUM (Lucania); ear of barley within beaded circle; rev. same, incuse. Fine and broad; rare; di. S. Size 17
47 —— Another; same in all respects, but dark.
48 —— Another. Extremely fine; thick di., also incused. Size 13
49 —— Duplicate. Poor.
50 —— Head of Ceres; rev. ear of barley, META. Misstruck, but fine; di. S.
51 NEAPOLIS (Campania); head of Ceres, necklace and earrings; rev. a bull with human face walking to l.; NEAPOL; all in hollow. Misstruck, fine; di. S.
52 —— Similar; bull to r.; NEAPOLITON; di.
53 —— Similar; varieties. 2 p
54 —— Drachm, and two copper. 3 p
55 PHILIP (Macedon); head laureated and bearded; rev. boy with palm on horseback; name in Greek; Clump planchet, but uncommonly sharp and fine; S. Tet. Size 15 x 12
56 PHOCIS; bull's head, front view; C. 2 p
57 SYRACUSE (Sicily); female head to r.; hair in net; with double border; SYRACUSION (in Greek), retrograde; rev. biga. Fine and remarkable tetradrachm.
58 —— Head of a woman; hair in net, bound with a string of pearls; around 4 dolphins and name of the city; rev. biga, Victory crowning the horses. Uncommonly fine; Tet. S.
59 —— Head of Proserpine, with necklace and earrings, name of the city, and 4 dolphins around; rev. a quadriga to l., Victory crowning the driver; in ex. suit of armor; MEDALLION. Extremely fine and valuable; decadrachm; S.
60 —— Same head as 58; rev. Polypus; S.; hemi-drachm. Very fine and rare.
61 —— Head of Pallas; rev. star of 8 points within a circle formed by two dolphins. Patinated and fine; thick, C. Size 18

Greek.

62 Syracuse (Sicily); Head, laureated and bearded; rev. eagle and thunderbolt; *C.* Patinated and *ex.* fine. Size 16
63 —— Head of Hercules in lion's scalp; rev. Pallas armed, striking to r.; in field owl; SYRAKOSION; and another; C. Fine. 2 p
64 —— Young head, diademed; rev. Victory conducting a biga. Inscription effaced, but the type perfect and extremely fine; a large copper coin, perhaps of Hiero I. Size 22
65 Hiero I. (King); head; rev. a horseman; name in ex. Patinated and fine; C. Size 17
66 —— Duplicate. Very fine.
67 Sinope (Paphalonia); head of Jupiter to r.; rev. eagle on a thunderbolt to l.; in the field Æ and *. Extremely fine, rare; C. Size 12
68 Tauromenium; rev. tripod; Thessalonica; rev. two goats butting; and others; struck for circulation in Campania, some with clusters of grapes, etc.; C. Poor. 25 p
69 —— Another unclassified lot of Greek copper coins; all fine and interesting. 10 p
70 —— Greek, and Greek Imperial coins. 25 p
71 Tarentum (Calabria); female head, diadem, and ear-rings; rev. cavalier riding to r.; to l. cornucopia; below, a dolphin; S. di. well preserved; rare type.
72 —— Taras on dolphin to l. holding a diota and cornucopia; rev. same, but with ins. under the horse. Extra fine, *rare.*
73 —— Same type, but with trident; and behind, head of Venus; rev. cavalier galloping to r. with lance. Extra fine; di. S.
74 —— Neptune seated; rev. Taras on dolphin, one hand raised, in the other a polypus; below the dolphin, a shell; broad, di. in fair condition, and excessively rare.
75 —— Varieties of the same (di); some with the horse going slow, others stepping, and on one, running at full speed; (rare); from fair to good. 7 p

Antique Coins.

76 TARENTUM (Calabria); Same as No. 71; rev. horseman with palm riding; l. below the horse, dolphin and tripod; with another *rare variety*; about as they were struck. One in Wellenheim brought 6 thalers. 2 p
77 TERINA (Bruttium); head of a female in casque; rev. Victory standing with palm; *S* di. well preserved. Rare.
78 THURIUM (Lucania); head of Pallas to r.; her helmet adorned with the monster scylla; rev. a bull charging to r.; in ex. fish; misstruck, but *fine*; S. di. Rare. Size 13
79 —— Same head; olive on helmet; rev. Taurus Cornupetus to l.; same size and condition.
80 —— Other didrachms; scylla on helmet; ordinary. 2 p
81 TYRE (Phœnicia); head laureated; (Baal?) rev. eagle on a rudder; various monograms and symbols; pierced, but very fine. Rare, tet. S.
82 VELIA (Lucania); head of Pallas; griffon on helmet; rev. lion walking to r.; in the field caduceus; in ex. (in Greek) VELETON; S. di. Fine.
83 —— Same; sphinx on helmet; rev. lion to l. devouring his prey; equally fine; di. S.
84 —— Repetition of last.
85 —— Duplicate of 81 and 84; except on former a harpie above the lions; both good. 2 p
86 —— Female head; rev. lion springing on the back of a stag, and another lion walking; good, di. 2 p
87 —— Female head; rev. owl; drachma. 2 p
87* UNCLASSIFIED silver coins; 1 didrachm, and 4 drachma.
  5 p

ROMAN.

THE AS WITH ITS DIVISIONS.

88 FEMALE head with three turrets; nearly front view; long ringlets and ear ornaments; rev. bull walking to r. his head turned to the front; below, ROMA; above, 1 patinated, and in remarkable preservation considering the high relief of the figures. Size 44
89 As of the usual type; Janus' head and prow. Size 43

Denarii of Roman Families.

90 SEMIS; head of Hercules; below S.; rev. prow, above S; a noble coin; fit companion to 98.   Size 22
91 TRIENS, ●●●○ ; thunderbolt; rev. dolphin.   " 30
92 QUADRANS, ●●● ; same type as 90.   " 26
93 SEXTANS, ●● ; shell; rev. S   " 24
94 UNCIA, ● ; helmeted head; rev. prow; v. thick.   " 16

The series of the *Libralis* As, complete, and so good as to merit special notice; No. 88 is certainly a very rare and valuable coin, and in the Dimsdale sale (1824) brought 6 guineas.

95 SERIES from As to Uncia; large to small brass sizes; not easily completed.   6 p
96 As; reduced from the original *As gravis*, yet of unusual size for this type; (size 23); very fine, with small semis and sextans.   3 p
97 PARTS of the As.   7 p
98 As; large brass size.   2 p
99 SAME, with Roman copper rings; used as weights (?)   5 p

DENARII OF ROMAN FAMILIES.

100 ABURIA; head of Rome; rev. quadriga, M. ABURI. Very fine.
101 ACCOLEIA; laureated head; rev. the sisters of Phaeton changing into larch trees; (a pun upon the name of Lariscolus, who struck the coin). Ordinary.
102 ACILIA ; female head, SALVTIS; rev. Hygea standing. Ordinary.
103 AMILIA; veiled head (Vesta), PAVLLVS. LEPIDVS CONCORDIA; rev. a trophy; 4 figures near (Lepidus, Perseus and his sons); large size and extremely fine.
104 —— Duplicate of 103, with one of the Antonia family. Fine and rare.   2 p
105 —— Aretas kneeling; one hand extending a palm; by his side a camel, M. SCAVR. AEDCVR. EX. S.; rev. Jupiter in a quadriga holding a thunderbolt; below, scorpion, P. HYPSAE. AED. CUR. C. HYPSAE. COS. Extra fine.

Antique Coins.

106 ANTONIA; head of Marc Antony, bare, M. ANT. IMP. AVG. III. VIR. RPC. M. BARBAT. Q. P.; rev. head of Octavius, bare; CAESAR. IMP. PONT. III. VIR. P. C. Extremely fine and rare. Size 12

107 —— Eagle between two ensigns, LEG. XIV; rev. galley, M. ANT. AVG. III. VIR. R. P. C. Extra fine.

108 —— Varieties of this type; legions XV. and XIX. 3 p

109 —— Head of Jupiter; rev. victory in a quadriga, Q. ANTO BALB; serrated edge. Fine and rare.

110 ANTESTIA and Aurelia; the last very fine. 2 p

111 AQUILLIA ; young head in casque, VIRTVS III. VIR.; rev. a soldier standing assisting a woman on her knees, M. AQVIL M. FMM.; in ex. SICIL; serrated edeg. Extra fine.

112 AURELIA; head of Pallas, COTA; rev. Hercules in a car drawn by two Centaurs, M. AVREL ROMA, and another. Fine and rare. 2 p

113 —— Head of Vulcan, with cap and star, near a pair of tongs; rev. eagle on thunderbolt; in ex. L. COT; both sides within a wreath of olives; serrated edge. Fine and rare.

114 AFRANIA, and another. 2 p

115 BAEBIA; head of Rome, TAMPIL; rev. Apollo in a quadriga, M. BAEBI. Fine and rare.

116 CALPURNIA; head of Apollo laureated; rev. horseman going at full speed, C. PISU. FRVGI.

117 —— Same type, with the addition of CXVIII. Very fine.

118 —— Same, but CXXXI and CXVIII. Very fine. 2 p

119 CASSIA; veiled head (Vesta); behind, lamp; rev. Longinus in the robes of a priest, standing before an altar, in hand tablets, LONGIN. III. V.; ex. fine and rare.

120 —— Veiled head (Liberty), Q. CASSIVS LIBERT; rev. a round temple surmounted by a statue, in field; vase, and tablet.

Denarii of Roman Families. 9

121 CLAUDIA; laureated head of Diana, behind lyre rev.; priestess standing, in each hand a long flambeau; P. CLODIVI; also another of this family, different type. Fine; rare.   2 p

122 —— Same as last described, with one struck by C. Pulcher. Very fine.   3 p

123 COELIA; head of Rome; rev. biga, C. COILCALD; and another.   2 p

124 CIPIA; head of Rome, M. CIPI. ME, and others; rev. Castor and Pollux riding to r.   4 p

125 CORDIA; heads of the Deoscuri wearing their peculiar caps, above each a star; rev. a blind-fold female standing holding an even balance and lance, on her shoulder an owl; not worn, but the surface oxidized; with coins of the Cornelia and Crepusia family, same as described under those heads. Good.   5 p

126 CORNELIA (by Sylla); head of Rome, with long hair, necklace and earrings. L. MANLI, P. R. O. Q.; rev. Sylla crowned by Victory while standing in his triumphal car drawn by four horses; in ex. L. SVLLA, IMP.; with one struck by Marcellinus, having the head of Hercules with lion's skin, club, and shield, and one by Lentulus; all rare. Fine lot.   3 p

127 —— (by Lentulus) bearded head diademed; behind, sceptre C P R.; rev. sceptre with laurels, globe, and rudder, CN. LEN. Q. E. X. S. C., as it came from the die; with coins of the Furia and Minutia families. Fair and fine.   3 p

128 CREPUEIA; young head laureated; behind sceptre; rev. Cavalier with lance charging; P. CREPVSI and another variety of same type. Both very fine.   2 p

129 DOMITIA; with Jupiter in a quadriga and Victory in a biga; on the last a man piercing a lion, in the field Very good.   2 p

130 EGNATULEIA; Victory erecting trophy; quinarus. Rare.

131 FABIA; veiled female head; rev. Victory in a biga; in the field an ostrich; C. FABI, C. F. Fine and rare.

Antique Coins.

132 FLAMINIA; head of Rome; rev. Victory in biga; with one of the Fonteia family; rev. Cupid on a goat; rare. Both very good. 2 p

133 FONTEIA; young head laureated; M. FONTEI. CF; rev. Cupid riding a goat; the caps and stars of Castor and Pollux in the upper field; in ex. thunderbolt; all within a laurel wreath and beaded circle; with one of the Furia and Flaminia gens. Valuable lot. 3 p

134 FUFIA; two young heads accolated, the outer one laureted, the other with helmet; near the first, HO; the other VIRT; rev. two females standing, joining hands; to l. ITAL in monogram; to r. R—(Italy and Rome); in ex. CORDI, serrated edge; large size. Beautiful and rare.

135 FURIA; 'head of Janus, M. FOVRI, L. F.; rev. Pallas crowning a trophy, PHILI. ROMA.; in field,*', with one of the Julia family Bursio. Good coins, a little stained. 2 p

136 JULIA (Cæsar); elephant walking to r.; before him a serpent; in ex. CÆSAR; rare Pontifical implements, with one of the Junia *gens* (Brutus); one v. f.; the last stained. 2 p

137 —— Another, same type (the elephants supposed to refer to Cæsar's African campaign, and the Pontifical implements to his piety); as it came from the die, in this condition very rare.

138 JUNIA; head of Liberty, LIBERTAS; rev. Marcus Brutus walking with three lictors; in ex. BRVTVS, very fine; with one of the Julia family (Bursio). Ordinary. 2 p

139 LICINIA (Macer); young man launching a triple javelin; rev. Minerva in a quadriga, with one of the Memmua family (Quirinus.) 2 p

140 LUCRETIA; winged head of Pallas, TRIO; rev. the dioscurii on their horses, C. N. LVCR. ROMA; ex. fine; some of Licinia gens (Macer.) 2 p

Denarii of Roman Families.

141 MAMILIA; bust of Mercury; to l. caduceus and letter M.; rev. Ulysses, staff in hand at the moment when he was recognized by his dog, C. MAMIL LIMETAN; serrated edge. Ex. fine; rare.

142 MARCIA; head of Apollo (by some honor); laureated; rev. nude figure of Silenus, with skin bottle full of wine on his shoulder; behind, a small statue on a column; to l. L. CENSOR; with a rare coin of the Plautia family. Fair. 2 p

143 —— Same as last, with one of the Porcia family (Cato); both rare. Well-preserved. 2 p

144 —— Same of Marcia, with one of the Titia gens. Both fine. 2 p

145 —— Winged head of Pallas, LIBO; rev. Castor and Pollux riding to r., and one of the Titia gens. 2 p

146 MARIA; head of Ceres; rev. two oxen yoked; above XV; and one of Titia. 2 p

147 MEMMIA; head of Ceres, C. MEMMI. C. F.; rev. a captive on his knees bound to a trophy, C. MEMMIVS, IMPERATOR; large and very fine. Rare.

148 MINUCIA; head without beard in a fine helmet; rev. two soldiers fighting; a third down; in ex. Q. THERM. MF.; ex. fine. Rare.

149 NAEVIA; diademed female head (Venus), with necklace and ear-rings; rev. Victory in a Trigæ; c., NAE, BA; above, CCXV. Ex. fine.

150 NORBANA; head of Venus; rev. fasces between caduceus and ear of wheat, broken; and one of the Papiria gens. 2 p

151 PAPIRIA; head of Rome; rev. small figure on a column between two ears of barley; priest advancing. Ordinary, but very rare.

152 PLANCIA; head of Diana, with the Pileus of Mercury, C. N. PLANCIVS, AED, CVR; rev. stagg; to l. bow with one of the Papiria gens (griffon). Both in ordinary condition, but rare. 2 p

153 PLAUTIA; head of Medusa; full face, L. PLAVTIVS; rev. Aurora in air between four coursers, PLANCVS. Large and ex. fine.

Antique Coins.

154 PLAUTIA. Turreted head (Cybele), A. PLAVTIVS. AED.
CVR. SC.; rev. Bacchus on one knee holding his
camel and extending a branch of olives, BACCHIVS
JVDAEVS; extremely fine, and one of the Poblicia
gens; Hercules strangling a lion. Ordinary.   2 p

155 POMPEIA; head of Rome; to l. vase; rev. a tree with
three birds shown; under it Faustulus standing by a
she wolf giving suck to the founders of Rome;
another, head of Neptune. Both uncommon.   2 p

156 POMPONIA; head of Apollo, Q. POMPONI. MVSA; rev.
Hercules Musagetes playing on a lyre, HERCVLES
MVSARVM.   Rare.

157 PORCIA; winged head of Pallas, P. LAECA. ROMA;
rev. soldier laying his hand on the head of a citizen;
a victor standing by with arms.   Fine and very rare.

158 POSTUMIA; bust of Diana, with her Attributes; in the
field the head of a stag; rev. an altar on a mountain
top, between a priest and a bullock; A. POST—N-
ALBIN.   Extra fine.

159 —— Same; equally fine, with one of the Rubria gens;
also fine.   2 p

160 —— Bare head of Postumius the Consul; rev. ALBINI-
BRVTI F, written within a crown of wheat. *Extra
fine and rare.*

161 —— Head of a woman, veiled; HISPAN; rev. man in
toga raising his hand over a Roman eagle; to r. fasces
and axe; serrated.   Extra fine and rare.

162 PROCILIA; head of Juno Sospita, in goatskin coif; rev.
same, in a toga, with arms, as represented in her temple
at Lanuvium; serrated edge.   Extra fine and rare.

163 —— Laureated head of Jupiter; rev. Juno Sospita
striking to r. with her lance, at her feet a serpent.
Extra fine and rare.

164 RENIA; head of Rome; rev. biga drawn by goats, and
one of the Rutilia family.   Very fine.   2 p

165 RUBRIA; laureated head of Jupiter; rev. triumphal car,
with horses; obv. misstruck. Extra fine, with one of
the Sentia gens.   Very fine.   2 p

166 RUTILIA; head of Rome; rev. biga; extra fine, with one of the Scribonia gen. Very fine. 2 p
167 SENTIA; head of Rome; rev. Jupiter in quadriga; L SATVRN, and one of the Tituria gens. 2 p
168 SCRIBONIA; diademed head of Fortune BON-I-VENT LIBO; rev. an altar, to which is attached two lyres and a garland of flowers, PVTEAL—SCRIBON, and one with the rape of the Sabines (Tituria). Very fine. 2 p
169 SERGIA; head of Minerva, necklace and ear-rings; rev. Marcus Sergius Silus on horseback, with his weapon and the head of an enemy in his left hand. Very fine, and one of the Vibia gens. 2 p
170 SERVILIA; head, without beard, in casque, RVLLI; rev. Victory, with palm in biga; and one of Vibia. Both fine. 2 p
171 —— Head to r.; rev. the Dioscuri, mounted, their horses starting in opposite directions, C. SERVILI, M F., with one of the Tituria gens (SABIN). 2 p
172 THORIA; head of Juno Sospita; rev. bull leaping—THO-RIVS—BALBVS. Very fine.
173 TITURIA; head of Tatius; rev. rape of the Sabine girls, and heaping shields on Tarpeia, with one; rev. temple. Valuable lot. 3 p
174 TULLIA; a fine coin of this family, with a duplicate of the Tituria (rape of the Sabines). 2 p
175 TITIA; head of Bacchus; rev. Pegasus, Q. TITI, with one of Valeria. Both fine. 2 p
176 VALERIA; bust of Victory, winged; rev. Mars standing; to r. ear of barley, to l. Apex; and a rare Quinarius SABIN. 2 p
177 VIBIA; head of Pan, PANSA; rev. Jupiter Axur (radiated) seated—C. VIBIVS C. F CN JOVIS AXVR. Extra fine and rare.
178 —— Head of Apollo, laureated, PANSA; rev. Pallas in quadriga, C-VIBIVS; and another. 2 p
179 —— Head of Minerva; rev. Hercules, standing; and another. 2 p
180 —— Duplicates of 178, and Titia. 2 p

Antique Coins.

181 VOLTEIA; head of Pallas; rev. Cybele in a car drawn by two lions; and others; two Quinarie.   6 p

ROMAN IMPERIAL COINS.
(*In Silver and Copper.*)

AUGUSTUS.

182 BARE head to l.; rev. Victory on globe, CÆSAR—DIVI; S. Fine and rare.

183 —— Head to r.; vev. capricorn (his horoscope); AVGVS-TVS; S. Fine and rare.

184 —— Same; rev. bull charging to l.; IMP. X; S. Very fine, rare.

185 —— Same; rev. bull charging to r. Fair, S.   2 p

186 HEAD, with spiked crown; rev. eagle; beautiful; and one equally fine; rev. altar, PROVIDENT; both perfectly patinated; second size or M. B.   2 p

187 —— Same as last (altar), with one of Nemausus (crocodile chained to a palm tree). Fine.   2 p

188 VARIETIES, M. B.   4 p

TIBERIUS.

189 HEAD, laureated: rev. Tiberius, as high pontiff, seated Extremely fine, S. Rare.

190 —— Same; not as good (Tribute money).

191 HEAD to l., bare, TI·CÆSAR-AVGVSTI-F-IMPERATOR; rev. Altar of Lyons between two Victories; medallion (size 21) in mixed metals containing silver; modern, but certainly as old as the Paduans, and valuable as a work of art.

ANTONIA AND GERMANICUS.

192 OF these—(wife and son of Drusus, Sen.)—one each. Very fine, M. B.   2 p

AGRIPPINA (*wife of Germanicus*).

193 HEAD of Agrippina to r., AGRIPPINA-MF-GERMAN-ICI-CÆSARIS ; rev. TI-CLAVDIVS-CÆSAR AVG GERM-PM-TR-P-IMP. P P. ; in the middle S.C., in the field countermark N-CAPR-G.B. ; partly patinated, and in perfect preservation, and rare. Size 22

NERO AND DRUSUS (*sons of Germanicus*).

194 HEADS of Nero and Drusus in cornucopias, crossed; between them, a caduceus upright ; rev. ins., and in the middle S. C. G. B. ; in excellent preservation and fairly patinated. Very rare. Size 22

CALIGULA.

[Caius was nicknamed *Caligula* because he, in common with the soldiers, wore the *Caligla*, a strong, coarse shoe.]

195 PIETY, veiled, seated, in one hand a patera, her left arm resting on a little statue, C. CÆSAR AVG—GERMANICVS-PM-TR-POT. ; rev. three figures sacrificing before a temple, one supposed to be the Emperor ; the temple is wreathed with flowers—DIVO AVG-S-C-G. B.; brown patination, scarcely at all worn. Very rare. Size 21

196 HEAD ; rev. Vesta seated ; beautiful. M. B.
197 —— Same, with one of Claudius ; same size. Fine. 2 p
198 —— Same, with first brass of Livia (Julia), wife of Augustus ; rev. a carpentum drawn by two mules. Rare, but poor, and with others, mostly rare, all sizes. 12 p

CLAUDIUS.

199 HEAD, laureated, to r. ; rev. Hope walking to l., in one hand a flower, SPES. AVG G. B. Fine, and extremely rare. Size 22
200 —— Same ; modern, of first-rate quality ; a Paduan, Same size and type.
201 HEAD to l. : rev. Liberty standing ; with others, all sizes, from second to very small. Rare lot. 8 p

16   *Antique Coins.*

NERO.

202 HEAD to r., laureated; rev. the Emperor seated on an estrade, assisted by four attendants (CONG II.) DAT-POP; slightly corroded on rev., but still a very fine coin. G. B.   Extra rare.   Size 22

203 —— Same; rev. temple of Janus; brown patination. G. B.   Fine, and very rare.   Size 22

204 DUPLICATE of 203.

205 HEAD to l. laureated; rev. triumphal arch, on it a quadriga between two Victories; a light brown patination, without the least trace of wear. G. B. Very rare type, and desirable.

206 MEDALLION of silver or tetradrachm, struck at Antioch; obv. laureated head; rev. eagle. Extremely fine (fine silver).   Size 14

207 DENARIUS; rev. eagle between two standards. Very fine, rare.

208 HEAD to r. and l.; different reverses; with one Paduan, and one very small, having an actor's table with vase, crown, mask, griffon, etc. Rare.   4 p

GALBA.

209 HEAD, laureated; rev. Victory; obverse fine, reverse poor; G. B.   Rare.   Size 22

210 PADUAN, G. B. and genuine M. B. Fine.   2 p

OTHO AND VITELLIUS.

211 HEAD of Otho; rev. head of the Empress; medallion (size 24); with one first brass; both modern. Fine.
                                                     2 p

212 HEAD of Vitellius; rev. Jupiter seated, IVITER VICTOR. Very fine and rare denarius.

213 PADUAN; two varieties; G. B.   2 p

VESPASIAN.

214 DENARIUS; rev. female, holding a branch, seated in a high back chair; COS VI. Very fine and rare.

Roman Imperial Coins.

215 DENARIUS; rev. Victory crowning a military ensign; and another. 2 p
216 —— Same; COS VIII.; head to r.; rev. two oxen in a yoke. Extra fine; an interesting coin.
217 HEAD to l., laureated; rev. the Colisseum which he caused to be built, and named for his son Titus; a small piece broken out of one side injuring it but little; an excellent picture of the Emperor and his great edifice; G. B. Extremely rare.
218 —— Same; rev. the Emperor standing, one foot on a globe, in one hand the parazonium (or baton), the other resting on his spear; on the ground a woman, seated; between them a palm tree; JVDEA CAPTA; G. B. In fair preservation, and very rare. Size 21
219 FORTUNE, standing; G. B., and others M. B. Fine lot. 3 p

TITUS (*son of Vespasian*).

220 HEAD, laureated; rev. female seated; S. Fine.
221 HEAD to l.; rev. Hope standing; G. B. Fine and rare. Size 22
222 —— With different reverse; M. B. Good and fine. 3 p

DOMITIAN (*Brother of Titus*.)

223 HEAD, laureated; rev. Sella Curulis, and crown; S. Fair.
224 —— Same; rev. Pallas, walking; S. Rather poor.
225 SECOND size copper; all different. Fine and rare. 4 p
226 PADUAN; rev. religious ceremonies before a temple; medallion and as of the first brass size. 2 p

NERVA (*a Senator, created Cæsar*).

227 HEAD, laureated; rev. two hands joined, holding a Roman eagle planted on the prow of a galley; CONCORDIA EXERCITVM; S. Fine denarius, rare type.
228 —— Same; rev. two hands joined; M. B. Fine.

TRAJAN (*a Spaniard*.)

229 DENARIUS; obv. laureated head; rev. half nude female. seated in a high-back chair holding a branch; before her a Dacian kneeling, S. P. Q. R.; OPTIMO PRINCIPI; as fine as when struck. S.

18   *Antique Coins.*

230 Denarius; rev. female with rudder and cornucopia; S Fine.
231 Head, laureated; rev. female standing with Caduceus and Cornucopia, G. B. Very fine.   Size 22
232 —— Same; with another same size; rev. the collosseum. In fair preservation for so rare a coin.   2 p
233 —— Second size, one patinated and as fine as possible.
                                                        2 p

Hadrian, and Sabina (*his wife.*)

234 Head, laureated; rev. the Emperor and a woman joining hands, FELICITAS, AVG; with one of Sabina; rather poor, but rare. S.   2 p
235 Head of Hadrian, laureated; rev. Rome seated on a cuirass holding hasta and parazonium, COS. III; and one of Sabina; both beautiful denari; S.   2 p
236 Denarius of Sabina; G. B. of Hadrian; different rev.
                                                        2 p
237 Head, laureated; Justice standing with scales, AEQVITAS, AVG; patinated and v. fine; valuable G. B.
238 —— Same; different reverses; G. B. from size 22 to 17.   3 p
[From this date downwards the size of the Sestertiut (Great Brass) is very uneven, but generally much reduced.]

239 Head to left; rev. a galley full of sailors rowing to left; above, FELICITATI, AVG.; and below COS. III., PP.; M. B. in excellent preservation and v. rare; with three others almost equally rare. Fair.   4 p

Antinous (*Hadrian's favorite.*)

240 Bust of Antinous draped; head bare; Greek legend; rev. Mercury with Pegassus; a beautiful medallion; perfectly patinated and believed to be antique; of the highest rarity; bronze.   24 Size.

Aelius (*adopted by Hadrian.*)

241 Head to r. bare; ver. Concord seated; denarius. Extremely fine and *very rare.*

Antoninus Pius.

242 HEAD laureated to r.; rev. Vesta standing holding a simpulum (sacred vessel with long handle), and the palladium; COS. III.; ex. fine; S. Rare.

243 —— Same; rev. Ceres standing with ears of wheat and cornucopia. Equally fine. S.

244 —— Same; rev. bare head of Aurelius; beautiful; S Rare.

245 —— Same; rev. catafalque, CONSECRATIO; extremely fine. S.

246 —— Same; rev. Italy seated on a globe with Hasta and Cornucopia; large G. B. (size 22); patinated and fine. Rare.

247 OTHERS of same size. Ordinary.   3 p

248 SECOND size; brass coins. Fine.   3 p

249 ANOTHER lot with other Emperors.   10 p

Faustina, Sen. (*wife of Antonino.*)

250 HEAD to r.; rev. Hexastyle temple (six columns); adorned with statues, AED. DIV. FAVSTINAE; beautiful and rare. S.

251 —— Same; reverses various; denari. Ordinary.   3 p

252 —— Same; rev. Eternity standing; G. B. and M. B.; patinated. Fine.   2 p

253 OTHERS with M. Aurelius. Good lot.   5 p

Marcus Aurelius.

254 HEAD; rev. woman feeding a serpent, rising from a round altar. Extra fine. S.

255 —— Same; rev. Liberality standing; Justice seated, and Providence standing. Fine. S.   3 p

256 —— Same; rev. like 254, G. B. (size 21); perfectly patinated and very fine. Rare in this condition.

257 ANOTHER G. B.; same type; fine light green patination. Fine and rare.

258 OTHER G. B. and M. B. Fine lot.   5 p

Antique Coins.

FAUSTINA, JUN. (*wife of Aurelius.*)

259 HEAD; rev. Juno accompanied by a peacock. Very fine. S.
260 —— Same; rev. woman with four children, FECVN-DHE. S.
261 OTHER denariis. Ordinary. 2 p
262 G. B. and M. B. Fine and rare lot. 3 p

LUCEUS VERUS (*Emperor with Aurelius.*)

263 BEARDED head, bare; rev. Providence standing. Extremely fine denarius. S.
264 DENARIUS of Aelius Verus, father of L. Verus. Extra fine and rare.
265 BARE head of Verus; rev. Aurelius and Verus standing joining hands, fine and perfectly patinated; a rare type. G. B.   Size 21
266 HEAD *laureated*; rev. Fortune seated; small brass; as fine as when struck. Rare.

LUCILLA, (*wife of Verus.*)

267 HEAD; rev. Concord seated. Extra fine, S.
268 —— Same; rev. Venus standing. Fine, S.
269 FIRST and second brass; fine to poor. 5 p

COMMODUS, AND CRISPINA (*wife of Commodus.*)

270 HEAD of Commodus, covered with a lion's scalp; rev. within a wreath, club and HERCVL, ROMAN AVGV. Fine denarius, and very rare. S.
271 HEAD of Crispina; rev. Venus standing with hasta and apple. Very fine. S.
272 G. B. coins of Coms. and Cris.; with one denarius. 3 p

SEPTIMUS SEVERUS.

273 HEAD; rev. Cybele, with thunderbolt and spear, riding a lion to r., INDVLGENTIA AVGG IN CARTH A rare type, and very fine. S.

Roman Imperial Coins.

274 HEAD; rev. Victory passing to l., holding a garland; poised on a base, a round shield; and another as it came from the die. S. 2 p

275 OTHERS; silver and copper. 3 p

JULIA DOMNA (*wife of Severus.*)

276 HEAD; JVLIA PIA FELIX AVG; rev. Venus; S. Extra fine.

277 —— Same; rev. Diana; S. Very fine.

278 BUST, draped; ver. Venus Victrix; Patinated and fine. M. B.

GETA AND CARACALLA (*Sons of Sept. Sev. and Julia.*)

279 HEAD of Geta; rev. the Prince standing near a trophy; S. 3 p

280 HEAD of Caracalla; young man near two standards; S. 2 p

PLAUTILLA, HELIOGABALUS, AND JULIA MAESA.

281 HEAD of Plautilla (wife of Caracalla); rev. the Emperor and Empress joining hands; Good and rare type. S.

282 DENARII of Heliogabalus; as they came from the die. S. 2 p

283 HEAD of Julia Maesa, aunt to Heliogabalus; fine; Rare. S.

ALEXANDER, AND JULIA MAMAEA (*his mother.*)

284 HEAD of Alexander; rev. Victory standing writing on a shield, VOTX; a rare type; as it came from the die. S.

285 —— Same; rev. Ceres and another. Fine, S. 2 p

286 HEAD laureated; the Sun standing, his right hand raised, in his left a ball; as sharp as when it fell from the die, and beautifully patinated; bright green; G. B. Size 17 x 20.

287 —— Same; rev. Ceres standing; Modius at her feet; nearly as fine as last; G. B.

22   *Antique Coins.*

⎧ 288 Others of Alexander, G. B and M. B.   Good coin.   5 p
⎨ 289 Denarius and G. B. of Julia Mamaea.   Fair.   2 p
⎩ 290 Other G. B. of Julia and Alexander.   Very good.   4 p

Maximinus.

291 Head laureated; rev. Providence standing; beautiful;
    and another; S.   2 p
292 —— Same; rev. Hygea seated, SALVS. AVGVSTI;
    G. B.; extra fine and perfectly patinated. Very rare.
293 Another first brass of this type; beautiful bright
    green patination, and sharp as when struck. A gem.
294 —— Same; rev. FIDES MILITVM. Extra fine, G. B.
295 Others of the first size.   Fine to poor.   4 p

Maximus and Balbinus.

296 Head of Maximus bare; rev. implements used in relig-
    ious ceremonies—vase, simpulum, lastral, praefericu-
    lum, etc.; PIETAS. AVG; G. B. Fine and rare.
297 Laureated head of Balbinus; rev. Providence, stand-
    ing, holding baton and cornucopia; PROVIDENTIA-
    DORVM-S C.; patinated and fine; G. B. Very rare.

Gordian III.

298 Head; rev. different; S. All fine.   5 p
299 —— Same; rev. the Emperor walking to r.; G. B.
    Beautiful.
300 —— Same; rev. Eternity personified; G. B. Equal to
    last.
301 Others of first size; good and poor.   4 p

Philip, sen. (*the Arab*).

302 Head, radiated; rev. the young Prince on horseback; S.
303 Head, laureated; rev. FIDES MILITVM; a fine thick
    first brass patination, nearly perfect. Rare.
304 Duplicate, not patinated, as it fell from the die.
305 Another G. B.; rev. SALVS; patinated and fine.

OTACILLA (*wife of Philip I.*)

HEAD to r.; Concord seated, holding a patera and horn of plenty; G. B. Patinated, and *extra fine*.

PHILIP, JR. (*son of Philip and Otacilla*).

HEAD, radiated; rev. Prince standing, with ball and hasta; S. Extremely fine.

HEAD, laureated, and head bare to r.; two first size brass coins. Patinated, and very fine. 2 p

OTHERS this size; father and son. Fine to fair. 3 p

TRAJANUS DECIUS, AND ETRUCILLA (*his wife*).

HEAD, radiated; rev. female standing, holding a purse and cornucopia, VBERITAS AVGG; as it came from the die; S. Rare type.

HEAD, laureated; rev. the Province Dacia standing, holding the ass-headed standard; beautiful light green patination; as sharp as when struck; G. B. Rare.

OTHERS, same size, patinated. Fair. 4 p

DIADEMED head of Etruscilla on a crescent; rev. Fecundity personified; silver; as it came from the die. Rare.

HERENINUS ETRUSCUS (*son of Decius*).

BARE HEAD; rev. the Prince standing, PRINCIPI JVVENTVTIS-SC.; G. B. Very fine and extremely rare; and same type in silver, except the head is radiated. 2 p

TREBONIANUS GALLUS.

HEAD, radiated; rev. Eternity personified as a female, standing, holding a bird on a globe; S. Extremely fine, rare.

ANOTHER silver and first brass, well patinated; rev. Liberty standing, with her Attributes. A very rare type. 2 p

HEAD, laureated; rev., within wreath, EX VOTIS DECENNALIBVS, S. C; G. B. Extra fine and rare.

Antique Coins.

Volusianus.

318 Head, radiated; rev. Peace, with olive branch and hasta; S. Beautiful. 2 p

319 Head, laureated; rev. female leaning on a cippus, with caduceus and hasta; G. B. Fair.

320 Others, same size; ordinary. 2 p

Valerian, Gallienus, Salonina, and Postumus.

321 Denarius of each (2 of Postumus), as they were coined; good reverses. 5 p

Victorinus, Claudius II., Aurelian, Tacitus Probus, Carinus, Numerianus, Diocletian, Maximianus, Maxculus, and Licinius.

322 A selection to represent each of these Emperors in brass coins of good quality. 20 p

[This takes the series to the time of Constantine, at which point we shall discontinue the Catalogue, making coins of the Constantines the last lot.]

Constantine the 1st and his Sons.

323 Patinated and characteristic copper coins of several members of the family. 15 p

[All that follow are copper.]

324 Coins of the later Emperors; selected. *All fine.* 15 p

325 —— Similar; many patinated and fine. 50 p

326 Duplicate lot of the 12 Cæsars, and other early Emperors; many good G. B. in the lot. 30 p

327 Miscellaneous ancient coins; some Greek imperial. 65 p

328 —— Similar; all Roman. Very ordinary. 50 p

329 —— Similar " " 50 p

330 —— Similar " " 100 p

331 —— Similar " " 110 p

332 —— Similar " " 127 p

333 Coins of Gothic Emperors from John Zimisces; several fine and uncommon; Eg. that of Johannes with the

Antique Christian Medals. 25

bust of Christ, full face, and nimbused; ✠ EMMAN-
OVIIL; rev. cross on 3 steps; IS-XS-BAS-ILE-
BASILE, etc., etc. 27 p
334 Two copper coins; one Bactrian the other Persian; well
preserved and interesting. Size 16
335 BEAUTIFUL silver coin of Sapor II.; highly ornamented
bust to r.; Sassanidan legend; rev. fire altar, on
which is a human head; on each side a Magian standing; Sassanidan legend (Mionet V. 695, 19; Wellenheim 7,102). Much the finest that I have seen. (Rare
5). Size 17
336 ARSACES XV.; head in helmet, with "lobster back;" rev.
archer. Fine drachm; rare.
337 Two extremely fine and rare Sesterti of Heraclius; head;
rev. cross. Size 6

A FEW JEWISH COPPER COINS.

338 SIMON; pot of manna; Samaritan ins. Size 11
339 HEROD Agrippa; obv. tabernacle; rev. three ears of
barley. Rare. (Well. 6,996).
340 JOHN HYRCANUS; Samaritan ins. within a wreath of laurel;
rev. cornucopia. In fine preservation, but misstruck.
(Mionet, rare 4).
341 ALEXANDER; star or flower with 6 points or leaves, and
two others, unknown; one with palm tree extremely
small; perhaps a coin of the somewhat uncertain denomination known as the "Widow's mite." 3 p

ANTIQUE CHRISTIAN MEDALS.

342 HEAD of Christ; Hebrew ins.; rev. Hebrew ins. in 5
lines; a patinated copper medal with serrated edge.
Size 22
343 —— Similar medal. Size 17
344 BEARDED head, horns projecting in front; rev. Hebrew
ins. Copper. Size 22
345 HEAD, with a ram's horn; Hebrew ins. on collar and rev.
Same size.

[Medals similar to the above are in the Ashmole library at Oxford,
England, and have occasioned prolonged and curious conjectures.]

American Coins.

It is argued that, as the head of Christ on the first two are without the nimbus which is found on all such heads after the 7th century, they were made previous to that date. One exactly like 343 was found in 1812 in Cork, on the site of an ancient monastery, contemporaneous with the introduction of Christianity into Ireland.]

345*HEAD of Christ, nimbused, I—N; rev. Hebrew ins. in 5 lines. A very fine old Medal. Size 64

AMERICAN COINS.

COLONIAL.

1652.

346 PINE tree shilling, MASATHVSETS. Very fine. Size 16
347 —— Same; small planchet. Fine. Size 15

1721 to '23.

348 LOUISIANA cents; two letter L's salterwise; one of each date. Rather poor. 2 p
349 ROSA-Americana penny (struck for two-pence); laureated head George I.; rev. rose; motto in schedule; date 1722. Circulated, but very fair.
350 ROSA-Americana half-penny (penny); same variety and date. Nearly uncirculated.
351 FARTHING of this date and variety; uncirculated. Rare.
352 HALF-PENNY; like 350. Equally fine.
353 —— Same, 1723; a crown above the rose; motto in a schedule. Extremely fine, rare.
354 PENNY, without date (rare); others, 1722; with half-pennies from poor to good. 12 p

1773 to '83.

355 VIRGINIA half-pennies, 1773. Fine to poor. 4 p
356 GEORGIUS Triumpho; half-penny; laureated head of George III.; rev. Liberty seated behind a paling, etc.; 1783; uncirculated. Very rare.
357 —— Another. Very fine.

Coins of the United States.

358 NOVA Constellatio, 1783; varieties, but little circulated; weak impressions. 3 p
359 WASHINGTON and Independence; with cent of the same date (1783) struck in France, "Unity States," and one with two heads of Washington; 5 varieties and pieces. Fine.
360 DUPLICATES of all the foregoing (1783). 13 p
361 CHALMERS' Annapolis sixpence, 1783; pierced, but better than usually found. Very rare.

1787 to '88.

362 MASSACHUSETS cents, one of each date. Fine, but dark. 2 p
363 —— Same; a variety, 1787; horn on eagle's head; same condition. Rare.
364 —— Same; cent and half-cent, 1788, latter pierced.
365 NEW JERSEY cent, 1787, large and small planchets, size 17 and 20. Fine. 2 p
366 CONNECTICUT cents, both dates; variety, with duplicates of the foregoing; Franklin and Vermont cents. 20 p
367 ELECTROTYPE copies of rare Granby and Washington cents. 3 p
368 KENTUCKY cent, without date; hand with scroll and inscription, "Our Cause is Just;" edge plain. Uncirculated.
369 WASHINGTON cent of 1791, large eagle; and token, "Success to the United States." Poor. 2 p
370 LIBERTY and Security half-penny, small size, lettered edge, 1795. Ex. fine and rare.

COINS OF THE UNITED STATES.

1793.

371 CENT; head of Liberty; rev. endless chain. Very fair, rare.
372 —— Same; rev. wreath. Not as good.

1794.

373 HALF-DOLLAR; pierced, fair. Scarce.
374 HALF-DIME; pierced, otherwise fine. Scarce.
375 CENTS; varieties. Very good. 2 p

American Coins.

1795.

376 EAGLE (10 D.); very poor. Scarce.
377 DOLLAR; flowing hair, slender wreath, and two leaves on laurel sprig. Circulated, but very good.
378 —— Same; thick wreath, bunches of three leaves. Same condition.
379 —— Same; fillet head; scratched planchet, but little rubbed. Scarce.
380 HALF-DOLLARS; considerably rubbed.   2 p
381 HALF-DIME; uncirculated. Very rare.
382 —— Same; nearly uncirculated; rev. scratched. Rare.
383 —— Same; good, but uncirculated.   3 p

1796.

384 DOLLAR; not much circulated, slight scratches. Scarce.
385 HALF-DOLLAR; *very fine* for date. Rare.
386 DIME; fine. Rare.

1797.

387 EAGLE (10 D.); rev. small eagle; nearly proof; splendid. Rare.
388 DOLLAR; six stars before the head of Liberty; very fine. Scarce.

1798.

389 DOLLAR; rev. large eagle. Circulated.
390 CENTS; slight varieties. Very good.   3 p

1799.

391 EAGLE (10 D.); *extremely* fine. Scarce.
392 —— Same; broken die; equally fine. Scarce.
393 DUPLICATE of this variety; very fine. Scarce.
394 HALF-EAGLE (5 D.); *extremely* fine. Scarce.
395 —— Same. Equally fine.
396 DOLLAR. Very fine.
397 —— Same. Equally fine.
398 —— Same. Fair and fine.   2 p

Coins of the United States.

1800.

399 DOLLAR; fine for date. Scarce.
400 —— Same. Circulated.
401 HALF-DIME; *very fine.* Scarce.

1801.

402 EAGLE (10 D.); *splendid;* nearly proof. Rare.
403 —— Same. Extremely fine.
404 —— Same. Equally fine.
405 DOLLAR. Fine.

1802.

406 HALF-EAGLE (5 D.); beautiful impression; *almost* uncirculated. Scarce.
407 DOLLAR (altered die of 1801). Fine.
408 HALF-DOLLAR; good for date. Scarce.

1803.

409 HALF-EAGLE (5 D.); die of 1802. Ex. fine.
410 DOLLAR. Circulated.
411 HALF-DOLLARS. Fair.
412 HALF-DIME; pierced, otherwise ex. fine. Rare.

1804.

413 CENT; very desirable; for date, fine. Rare.

1805.

414 HALF-EAGLE (5 D.) Extremely fine.
415 HALF-DOLLARS; one pierced. Ordinary.
416 QUARTER-DOLLAR; very good. Scarce.
417 DIME; fine. Scarce.

1806.

418 HALF-EAGLE (5 D.) Fine.
419 HALF-DOLLAR; scratched, but very fine.
420 —— Same; varieties. Circulated, but good.
421 —— Others. Ordinary.
422 QUARTER-DOLLARS. Ordinary.

1807.

423 HALF-EAGLE (5 D.) Very fine.
424 HALF-DOLLARS. Fair.   3 p
425 HALF-DOLLAR, quarter-dollar, and dime; ordinary; ($5c.)
     Sold as one lot.

1808.

426 QUARTER-EAGLE (2½ D.); a slight notch. Fine.
427 —— Duplicate. Fine.
428 HALF-DOLLAR; head to l. Fair.

1809 and 1810.

429 HALF-DOLLAR of each date. Ordinary.   2 p

1811 and 1812.

430 HALF-EAGLE (5 D.) of 1812; very fine. Scarce.
431 HALF-DOLLARS of each date. Fair.   2 p
432 —— Same of 1812. Very fine.   1 p
433 DIME of 1811; fair. Scarce.
434 CENT of 1812. Fair, but dark.

1813, 1814, and 1815.

435 HALF-DOLLAR of 1813 and '14. Fair.   2 p
436 HALF-DOLLAR and Quarter-Dollar, 75 cents, of 1815.
     Good; the lot.
437 CENTS of 1813 and 1814. Fair.   2 p

1816, 1817, and 1818.

438 HALF-DOLLAR of 1817 and 1818. Fair.   2 p
439 QUARTER-DOLLAR of 1818. Ordinary.
440 CENTS of each date. Fair.   3 p

1819.

441 HALF-DOLLAR. Fair.
442 QUARTER-DOLLARS; varieties. Ordinary.   2 p
443 CENTS; uncirculated; bright.   2 p

Coins of the United States.   31

1820.
HALF EAGLE (5 D.) Extremely fine, rare.
SET; half and quarter-dollar, dime and cent (86 cents).
  Good; the set.

1821 and 1822.
SET of 1821; half and quarter-dollar, dime, and cent
  (86 cents). Good; the set.
HALF and quarter-dollar and cent of 1822 (76 cents).
  Fair; the set.

1823.
HALF-DOLLAR. Very fine; scarce.
DIME and Cent. Fair; scarce.   2 p

1824.
HALF EAGLE (5 D.); extremely fine. Rare.
HALF-DOLLAR, quarter dollar, dime, and cent (86 cents).
  Ordinary; the set.

1825, 1826, 1827, and 1828.
HALF-DOLLAR of each date. Good.   4 p
QUARTER-DOLLAR of 1825 and 1828. Ordinary.   2 p
DIMES of 1825, 1827, and 1828. Very good.   3 p
CENTS of each date. Ordinary.   4 p

1829 and 1830.
HALF-DOLLAR of each date. Fine.   2 p
DIME and half-dime of 1829. Extremely fine.   2 p
DIME and half-dime of each date; 2 of each.   4 p
HALF-DOLLAR and quarter-dollar. Very fine.   2 p
QUARTER-DOLLAR; fine proof. Very rare.
HALF-DIME; brilliant proof. Rare.
DIMES. Ordinary.   2 p

1832, 1833, and 1834.
SET of 1832; half and quarter-dollar, dime and half-
  dime (90 cents). Ordinary set.
—— Same of 1833 (90 cents). Poor; the set.
—— Same of 1834. Very fine.

466 DIME and half-dime, 1834. Ordinary.   2 p
467 CENT ; perfect and uncirculated. Scarce.

1835 and 1836.

468 SET 1835 ; half-dollar, quarter-dollar, dime, and half-dime (90 cents). Fair ; the set.
469 —— Same of 1836 (90 cents). Very fine ; the set.
470 PATTERN DOLLAR, by *Gobrecht*, 1836. Fine proof impression, slightly scratched. Rare.

1837, 1838, 1839, 1840.

471 SET 1837 ; half and quarter-dollar, dime, and half-dime (90 cents). Fair ; set.
472 —— Same of 1838. Fair.
473 —— Same of 1839. Ordinary.
474 —— Same of 1840. Fine.

1841.

475 SET ; half-dollar, quarter dollar, dime, and half-dime (90 cents). Ordinary ; set.
476 CENT ; fine proof. Very rare.
477 HALF-CENT ; fine proof. Very rare.

1842, 1843, 1844, and 1845.

478 SET 1842 ; dollar, half, and quarter-dollar, dime, and half-dime ($1.90). The dollar very fine ; set.
479 —— Same of 1843 ($1.90). The dollar very fine ; set.
480 SEt of same without the dollar of 1844 (90 cents) ; set.
481 —— Same of 1845 (90 cents). Fair ; set.

1846.

482 DOLLAR, half, and quarter-dollar, and half-dime ($1.80). The dollar very fine, and the half-dime rare ; set.

1847, 1848, 1849.

483 DOLLAR of 1847 ; proof impression. Very slightly scratched ; rare.
484 SET ; half and quarter-dollar, dime, and half-dime (90 cents). Good ; the set.
485 —— Same of 1848 (90 cents). Very good ; the set.
486 —— Same of 1849 (90 cents). Very good ; the set.

Coins of the United States. 33

1850, '51, '52, '53, '54, and '55.

487 DOLLAR of 1850; proof impression; slightly circulated. Rare.
488 SET, half and quarter-dollar, dime, and half-dime (90 cents. Good; the set.
489 —— Same of 1851, with addition of 3 cents, silver, (93 cents). Fine; set.
490 —— Same as last of 1852 (93 cents). Fair; set.
491 —— Same of 1853 (93 cents). Fine; set.
492 QUARTER of 1853, without *arrow*-heads. Uncirculated; scarce.
493 HALF of 1854; N. O. Mint. Fine.
494 QUARTER of 1854; brilliant proof. Very rare.
495 DIME, half-dime (proof), and 3 cents. All fine. 3 p
496 SET, half-dollar, quarter dollar, dime, and half-dime, and 3 cents (93 cents) of 1855. Nearly all very fine; set.

1857.

497 SET, half-dollar, quarter dollar, dime, half-dime, and 3 cents (93 cents). Very fine; set.
498 CENT; old series; copper; fine proof; tarnished. Rare.
499 CENT; new series; nickel; fine proof; tarnished. Rare.

1861 and 1863.

500 SET, half and quarter dollar, and dime of 1861 (85 cents). Extremely fine; set.
501 —— Same of 1863; set.
502 HALF-DOLLARS of these and other dates. All fine. 4 p
503 HALF-DOLLARS of 1862 and 1865; quarters of 1841, 1856, and 1858; and dimes, half-dimes, and smaller U. S. coins (duplicates); intrinsic value $2.40; nearly all very fine. Many uncirculated; the lot.

PROOF SETS.

(With a few duplicates and patterns.)

1856.

504 NICKEL; cent.
SILVER; dollar, half-dollar, quarter-dollar, dime, half-dime, and 3 cents.
[Some of these are tarnised; the dollar is a brilliant proof, but altogether the set is not what it should be.]

1858.

505 NICKEL; cent.
  SILVER; dollar, half-dollar, quarter-dollar, dime, half-dime, and 3 cents. A fine and valuable set.

1859.

506 SAME as last; 7 pieces, all brilliant.
507 PATTERN half-dollar; head of Liberty; rev. 50 CENTS. Fine proof.

1860.

508 SAME as 506; 7 pieces, brilliant.
509 DOLLAR of the N. O. Mint. Very fine and rare.

1862.

510 SPLENDID proof set of this year; 7 pieces like those enumerated.

1865.

511 BRONZE; two cents; cent.
  NICKEL; three cents.
  SILVER; dollar, half-dollar, quarter-dollar, dime, half-dime, and 3 cents.
  GOLD; three dollars and one dollar. A splendid set of 11 pieces; intrinsic value, $5.99.
512 DUPLICATE 3 dollar piece; gold. Scarce.

1866.

513 BRONZE; two cents; cent.
  NICKEL; three cents.
  SILVER; dollar, half-dollar, quarter-dollar, dime, and half-dime, and 3 cents.
  GOLD; double-eagle, eagle, half-eagle, three dollars; quarter-eagle, and dollar. A beautiful set of 15 pieces; intrinsic value, $43.49.
514 DUPLICATE set of the bronze, nickel, and silver coins of this date; nine pieces.

Coins of the United States. 35

1867.

515 SAME as the full set of 1866, with the addition of a nickel 5 cent piece, making 16 pieces; value, $43.54.

516 PATTERN by *Longacre;* obv. head of Liberty coifed with plumes and starry garland; on ribbon UNION AND LIBERTY; legend, UNITED STATES OF AMERICA, 1867; rev. large **V.** on garnished shield; ins. IN GOD WE TRUST; struck in aluminum. Rare.

517 ANOTHER Pattern 5 cent piece; obv. shield, IN GOD WE TRUST; rev. 5 in circle of stars and rays. Pure nickel.

518 —— Same; obv. head of Liberty, UNITED STATES OF AMERICA, 1867; rev. 5 CENTS; within laurel wreath, IN GOD WE TRUST. Pure nickel.

1868.

519 FULL Set of the bronze, nickel, silver, and gold coins of this year; 16 pieces; intrinsic value, $43.54.

1869.

520 —— Same as last, lacking 3 cents; 15 pieces; value, $43.51.

1870.

521 FULL Set; bronze, nickel, silver and gold; 16 pieces; value, $43.54.

1871.

522 PROOF set of the bronze, nickel, and silver coins of this year. 10 p

523 SAME of the gold, from eagle to dollar; i. e. eagle, half-eagle, three dollars, quarter-eagle, and dollar, making 5 pieces; value, $21.50.

---

524 DOLLAR, 2 half-dollars, and 2 quarter-dollars of 1864 ($2.50). Fair; lot.

525 HALF-EAGLE of 1834 (new type); a good piece. Scarce.

526 MORMON gold coin, value 5 D.; obv. HOLINESS TO THE LORD, eye and other symbols; rev. C. S. L. C. P. C.; FIVE DOLLARS, 1850; two hands clasped. Pierced, but extra fine. Rare.

527 CAROLINA gold dollar. Bechtler; now scarce.

AMERICAN MEDALS.

MISCELLANEOUS.

528 VERNON SERIES; THE HON. EDWARD VERNON, ESQ. (this in ex.) HATH ONCE MORE REVIV'D THE BRITISH GLORY; the Admiral shown at three-quarter length, full face, right hand on hip, holding baton in left; behind him to r., a ship and FORT CHAGRE; to l., tree; rev. BY THE TAKING OF PORTO BELLO WITH SIX SHIPS ONLY, Nov. the 22d, 1739; a town and harbor in the form of a semi-circle; two large forts guarding the entrance, one in harbor; six ships lying in a double row before it. Very fine; rare variety; brass. Size 24

529 —— Same; the Admiral at full length, sword in hand; to r., ship; to l., fort; under the fort, HAVANA; the legend is ED. VERNON, ESQ., VICE-ADMIRAL OF THE BLUE; the reverse tells the same story as before in a different way. Extremely fine; brass. Size 23

530 —— Same; one side of this is the British coat-of-arms, the other is quite similar to the rev. of 528. Very fine, also rare. Size 24

531 —— Same; obv. much like 529, without the fort and ship, however, and with the addition of an anchor; the legend is, THE BRITISH GLORY, etc.; rev. AD. VERNON AND GEN'L OGLE TOOK CARTHAGENA BY SEA AND LAND; and, in ex., Ap'l 1, 1741; view of the town and harbor, with nine ships. Same size and equally fine.

Miscellaneous. 37

532 VERNON SERIES; THE SPANISH PRIDE PULLED DOWN, etc.; Don Blass kneeling before Admiral Vernon; two varieties, the Don on one knee and on *both* knees, with marked differences in the reverses. Both fine; size 24. 2 p

533 —— Same; ADMIRAL VERNON AND COMMODORE BROWN; the two officers at three-quarters length face to face; no ins., but a handsome ornament in the exergue; rev. the taking of Porto Bello—with another, not described. Equally fine; same size. 2 p

534 —— Same; ADM'L VERNON AND SR. CHALONER OGLE (and, in ex.,) WE LOOK FOR DON BLASS; rev. Carthagena, etc.; with another, which I think very rare. Same size. 2 p

535 —— Same; very pretty medals. Size 17. 2 p
[A full description would have shown that some of these medals differ from any described from Mr. Appleton.]

536 GULIELMUS PITT; bust in wig; rev. "The man who having saved the parent," etc. In red copper; an original impression; very fine and rare in this metal.
Size 26

537 —— Duplicate in brass. Very poor.

538 CAROLINA medal; Pallas standing with spear and palm; arms, armor, and several instruments used in the liberal arts lying to r. and l.; BOTH HANDS FILLED FOR BRITAIN; and in ex., GEORGE REIGNING; rev. a Queen watering a plantation of young palm trees; GROWING ARTS ADORN EMPIRE; and in ex., CAROLINE PROTECTING, 1736. Ex. fine; silver.
Size 25

539 —— Duplicate. Equally fine.

540 JOHAN DERK; a figure sitting on a monument, holding a cross and crown in one hand, and in the other a radiated baton; beside the monument a peasant leaning on a spade; a flat-country prospect; SVVM CVIQVE; rev. ins. in Latin; nine lines ending, ZWOLLA, 1 NOV., MDCCLXXXII.; by I. G. Holtzhey. Silver.
Size 21
[I suppose this to be one of Holtzhey's series of Dutch-American medals relating to the close of our revolutionary war; it is the first of the kind that has come in my way.]

541 FRANKLIN medals, 1706 and 1784; bust; rev. an angel standing above cloud, lightning descending. Fine proof; bronze. Size 29

541a —— Duplicate.

541b —— Same obv.; rev. ERIPUIT, etc., within wreath of oak. Fine proof, all by *Dupré*, and same size.

542 WASHINGTON medal by Westwood. An impression in tin; original and very rare. Size 26

[This is the only medal from Westwood's dies that I have seen in this metal. It is sharp and entirely uncirculated, but the metal appears to be disintegrating, and crumbles easily.]

543 —— Same; Bust; GEN'L GEORGE WASHINGTON; rev. within wreath, BORN FEB. 22, 1732; DIED DEC'R 14, 1799. Tin; uncirculated, but tarnished. Size 29

544 —— Duplicate. Equally fine.

545 —— Two others; badly tarnished. 2 p

546 —— Same; funeral medal; rev. urn. The well-known medal, so-called; original; silver. Very fine and rare. Size 18

547 —— Same; bust, bare; rev. bust of Lincoln, bare. Silver. Size 12

548 MEDAL; subject and history unknown; so far as I know, unique; two men standing with their *left* hands joined; one supports something on his shoulder by his right, while the other makes a gesture with his; WHERE LIBERTY DWELLS, THERE IS MY COUNTRY; in ex., OCT., the rest is obliterated; the rev. is plain, and appears to have had no impression; thick, very old planchet in lead or tin; much battered. Size 29 or 30

548* EDWIN FORREST; young head, bare; HISTRIONI OPTIMO EDDINO FORREST VIRO PRÆSTANTI MDCCCXXXIV.; under bust, C. C. W. Sr.; rev. Melpomēne seated; GREAT IN MOUTHS OF WISEST CENSURE; in ex., C. INGHAM, DEL. Splendid proof in silver (see illustration). Size 27

[I did not select this medal for the engraver until I had submitted it to the examination of my friend Mr. Edward Cogan, whose hearty commendation of the piece, in his judgment, equally interesting in subject and remarkable for rarity, decided my choice.]

Presidential. 39

549 GILBERT STUART; by the American Art Union. Fine
proof; bronze medal in case. Size 40
550 JOHN TRUMBULL; by same. Same size.
551 WASHINGTON ALLSTON; by same. Same size.
552 ZACHARY TAYLOR; by the State of Louisiana. A splendid *proof impression* of this well-known *but rare* "Pelican medal;" the only one in this condition that I have seen. Bronze. Size 48
553 BLACK Oak Agricultural Society, 1842; cotton tree and sheaf of wheat; rev. plough and ins.; an ugly hole punched through it. Thick silver medal; *very rare.* Size 24
554 WINYAH and All-Saints' Agricultural Society, 1857; plough; rev. sheaf of wheat; "Dr. J. R. Tucker, for Best Stallion," engraved on it. Silver medal; same size as last. Very fine and rare.
555 WORLD'S Fair, New York, 1853; view of the Crystal Palace; rev. globe. Proof in tin; rare. Size 47
556 JAMES BUCHANAN; rev. "The Union Must and Shall be Preserved." Very fine; tin. Size 38
557 JOHN C. FREMONT, the People's Choice for 1856. Very fine; tin; scarce. Size 38
558 ABRAHAM LINCOLN; medalet in silver on his assassination. Proof. Size 12

PRESIDENTIAL.

[All bronze and strictly fine proof.]

559 WASHINGTON; Evacuation of Boston; obv. bust; rev. Washington, with four officers, on horseback; the British embarking in boats in Boston Harbor; bronze proof, by Du Vivier. Size 40
560 —— Duplicate.
561 THOMAS JEFFERSON, 1801; bust; rev. two hands clasped, and a tomahawk and pipe crossed; PEACE AND FRIENDSHIP. Size 47
562 JAMES MADISON, 1809; bust; rev. same as last. By *Furst.* Size 40
563 JAMES MUNROE, 1817; bust; rev. same. By *Furst.* Size 40

564 JOHN QUINCY ADAMS, 1825 ; bust ; rev. as before. By
 Furst. Size 40
565 ANDREW JACKSON, 1829 ; bust ; rev. same. By Furst.
 Size 40
566 MARTIN VAN BUREN, 1837 ; bust ; rev. same. By Furst.
 Size 40
567 JOHN TYLER, 1847 ; bust, within wreath of oak ; rev.
 APRIL IV MDCCCXLI. Size 40
568 JAMES K. POLK, 1845 ; bust ; rev. MARCH IV MDC-
 CCXLV, within wreath, like last. Size 40
569 ZACHARY TAYLOR, 1849 ; bust ; rev. same as 561. Size 48
570 MILLARD FILLMORE, 1850 ; bust ; rev. citizen and Indian
 standing under the flag of the U. S.; agricultural
 scene, LABOR, VIRTUE, HONOR. By *Wilson &
 Ellis*. Size 48
571 FRANKLIN PIERCE, 1853 ; bust ; rev. same as last.
 Size 48
572 JAMES BUCHANAN, 1857 ; bust ; rev. agricultural scene,
 within circle ; above, two Indians, one scalping the
 other ; below, a squaw's head and Indian implements.
 By *Ellis*. Size 48
573 ABRAHAM LINCOLN, 1862 ; draped bust ; rev. same as
 last ; obv. by *Ellis*, rev. by *Wilson*. Size 40
574 ANDREW JOHNSON, 1865 ; bust ; rev. the two races (White
 and Red) joining hands in friendship before a monument surmounted by a bust of Washington. By
 Pacquet. Size 48

ARMY.

575 MAJ.-GEN. ZACHARY TAYLOR, for victory at Buena Vista,
 Feb. 22 and 23, 1847 ; spendid medal. By *Wright &
 Ellis*. Size 56
576 MAJ.-GEN. WINFIELD SCOTT ; March 9, 1848 ; for vic-
 tories in the Mexican war. By *Wright*. Size 56
577 —— Same ; for distinguished services in the battles of
 Chippewa and Niagara, July 5, 25, 1814. By *Furst*.
 Size 40
578 MAJ.-GEN. PETER B. PORTER ; for same victories.
 Size 40
579 BRIG.-GEN. ELEAZER W. RIPLEY ; for same victories.
 Size 40

Army—Navy. 41

580 BRIG.-GEN. JAMES MILLER; for the same. Size 40
581 BRIG.-GEN. JACOB BROWN; for the same. Size 40
582 MAJ.-GEN ZACHARY TAYLOR; for victories at Palo Alto and Resaca de la Palma, 1846. Size 40
583 —— Same; for victory at Monteray, Sept., 1846. Size 40
584 MAJ.-GEN. ANDREW JACKSON; for the victory of New Orleans, Jan. 8, 1815. By *Furst.* Size 40
585 MAJ.-GEN. WILLIAM HENRY HARRISON; for battle of the Thames, Oct. 5, 1813. By *Furst.*
586 GOV. ISAAC SHELBY; for services at the battle of the Thames, Oct. 5, 1813. By *Furst.* Size 40
587 COL. GEORGE CROGHAN; for his gallant defence of Fort Stephenson on Sandusky Bay, Aug. 2, 1813. By *Furst.* Size 40
588 MAJ.-GEN. HORATIO GATES; on the surrender of Gen. Burgoyne at Saratoga, Oct. 17, 1777. By *N. Gatteaux.* Size 34
589 COL. JOHN EDGAR HOWARD; for his services in the battle of Cowpens, March 9, 1781. Size 28
589*COL. WM. WASHINGTON; for same battle. Same size.

NAVY.

590 CAPT. JOHN PAUL JONES, of the "Bonne Homme Richard," for the capture of the English frigate "Seraph," Sept. 23, 1779. Size 35
591 CAPT. THOS. TRUXTUN; for services in the action between the frigates "Constellation" and "La Vengeance," March 24, 1800. Size 35
592 CAPT. STEPHEN DECATUR; for capture of the frigate "Macedonian," Oct. 25, 1812. By *Furst.* Size 40
593 CAPT. JACOB JONES; for the capture of the "Frolic," Oct. 18, 1812. By *Furst.* Size 40
594 CAPT. ISAAC HULL; for the capture of the "Guerreire," Jan. 29, 1813. Size 40
595 CAPT. WILLIAM BAINBRIDGE; for the capture of the British frigate "Java," Dec. 29, 1812. By *Furst.* Size 40

American Medals.

596 LIEUT. W. BURROWS; for the capture of the sloop "Boxer," Sept. 4, 1813. By *Furst.* Size 40
597 CAPT. JACOB LAWRENCE; for the capture of the British brig "Peacock," Feb. 24, 1813. By *Furst.* Size 40
598 LIEUT. EDW. R. McCALL; for the capture of the British sloop "Boxer," Sept. 4, 1813. By *Furst.* Size 40
599 CAPT. LEWIS WARRINGTON; for the capture of the British brig-of-war "Epervier," March 29, 1814. By *Furst.* Size 40
600 CAPT. JOHNSON BLAKELY; for the capture of the British sloop-of-war "Reindeer," June 28, 1814. By *Furst.* Size 40
601 CAPT. THOS. MACDONOUGH; for the victory on Lake Champlain, Sept. 11, 1814. By *Furst.* Size 40
602 CAPT. HENRY EAGLE; for same victory. By *Furst.* Size 40
603 LIEUT. STEPHEN CASSIN; for same. By *Furst.* Size 40
604 CAPT. JAS. BIDDLE; for the capture of the British sloop-of-war "Penguin," March 23, 1815. By *Furst.* Size 40
605 MAJ.-GEN. EDMUND P. GAINES; for his services in the Battle of Erie, Aug. 15, 1814. By *Furst.* Size 40
606 MAJ.-GEN. ALEXANDER MACOMB; for the Battle of Plattsburgh, Sept. 11, 1814. By *Furst.* Size 40
607 COM. CHARLES STUART; for the capture of the British sloops-of-war "Levant" and "Cyane," Feb. 20, 1815. By *Furst.* Size 40

CENTS, HALF-CENTS, TOKENS, CARDS, ETC.

608 CENTS; nearly a full set, with many duplicates. Poor. 164 p
609 HALF-CENTS; including a good 1811. 27 p
610 SHINPLASTERS; mostly of 1837. 40 p
611 Store cards; W. W. Wilbur's, in brass; fine proof, silver plated, with duplicates in copper and brass, etc. 17 p
612 SUTLERS' tokens; H. Rice, of McClernand's Brigade, Ill. Vols.; set, 50cts., 25cts., 10cts., 5cts. (dies by John Stanton, Cinn., O.); struck in thin brass; from size 16 to 10. 4 p
613 —— Same; 25cts. of E. E. Bedford, 127 N. Y. S. V. Rare.

Coins and Medals of Great Britain. 43

613* SAGE's tokens; Old Masonic Hall, and Chas. J. Bushnell; fine proofs; bronze. 2 p
614 POLITICAL, etc.; Jackson, Scott, Cass, Franklin Pierce, Lincoln, Hartford, Wide-Awake, etc. 10 p

COINS AND MEDALS OF GREAT BRITAIN.

ANGLO-SAXON AND ENGLISH TO VICTORIA.

615 EANRED, King of Northumberland, A. D. 808 to 827; obv. EANRED REX.; in the middle, anulet and dot; rev. MONNE ✠; in the middle a cross; stycae; small silver coin; black. R. R.
616 EDILRED REX; VIGMVND REX; EGBERT REX, etc.; same. 5 p
617 CANUTE (DANE); 1015 to 1035; profile; to l. sceptre, CNVT REX; rev. ERIMULFM. TOEOFR.; double cross in a circle, and four anulets with dots. Extra fine and rare penny.
618 EDWARD, the Confessor; 1042 to 1066; obv. bearded bust to r.; crown and sceptre; rev. cross with three crescents at each end; beautiful penny. Extremely rare.
619 WILLIAM I., Conqueror; 1066 to 1087; bust, full face; rev. PAXS, etc.; as fine as last.
620 RICHARD I., (Cœur de Lion); 1189 to 1196; obv. RICARDVS. REX. P., short cross; rev. PIC-TAVIE-NSIS. Extra fine and rare penny.
621 HENRY III., 1216 to 1272. Penny; fine.
622 EDWARD I., 1272 to 1307. Extra fine penny.
623 EDWARD III.; 1327 to 1377; groats struck at London; crowned bust; full face on a rose within a circle of dots; rev. long cross dividing the inscription in two circles, which is the type of all such money for several reigns; full size and weight, but bent and stained. 3 p
624 EDWARD IV., 1461; groats struck at York (EBORACI), London, Dublin (DVBILINI), and Waterford; one slightly broken. Fine lot, and very rare. 4 p
625 SCOTCH groats of David II. and Robert II., 1329; struck at Edinburgh and Perth. Very fine. 3 p

44 *Coins and Medals of Great Britain.*

626 HENRY VI., 1422 to 1461; fine London groat.
627 HENRY VII., 1485 to 1509; groat; profile to r. Poor.
628 HENRY VIII., 1509 to 1547; Irish groats, with the initial letter of a queen on each (A. J. R.) Fine.   3 p
629 EDWARD VI., 1547 to 1553; shilling (M. M. ton); the best one that I ever saw; a beauty, almost uncirculated. Rare.
630 MARY, 1553 to 1558; groat; bent and rubbed. Rare.
631 PHILIP AND MARY; shilling and sixpence for Ireland, their heads vis-a-vis; above, crown; rev. harp; base. Ordinary to fine.   3 p
632 ELIZABETH, 1558 to 1603; shilling, sixpence, and groat. Fair.   3 p
633 SAME; milled sixpence; very fine, rare; and one (1593) mint mark ton; nearly uncirculated. Rare.   2 p
634 SAME; poor sixpences, and rare Irish copper.   6 p
635 JAMES I., 1603 to 1625; shilling. Very fine.
636 SAME; engraved medalion heads of the King and his son Prince Charles (I.) " Give Thy judgment," etc. Uncommonly fine.
637 SAME; another like last; and sixpences.   4 p
638 CHARLES I., 1625 to 1649; half crown; M. M. ton. Uncommonly fine, rare.
639 SAME; half crown; different die. Fine.
640 SAME; shilling and sixpence; nearly uncirculated. Rare.
        2 p
641 ANOTHER shilling. Equally fine.
642 SHILLINGS, and Scotch and Irish coins.   5 p
643 COMMONWEALTH, 1649 to 1658; shilling and sixpence; the former very fine; both good.   2 p
644 CHARLES II., 1661 to 1685; coronation medal; obv. crowned bust; long hair in curls; order chain over a cape of Ermine; rev. the King seated, an angel crowning him; by *Thomas Simon*; a brilliant proof impression. *Very* rare, silver.   Size 18
645 —— Medal; heads of Charles and Katharine of Portugal, accolated; rev. nude figures on a cloud (Jupiter, Venus and Cupid), MAJESTAS-ET-AMOR; splendid proof; thick silver. Very rare.   Size 17

Anglo-Saxon and English to Victoria. 45

646 CHARLES II.; Medal in two pieces; bare bust; rev. a blighted tree bearing three crowns; the sun breaking through the clouds, TANDEM REVIRESCET; thin shells, silver. Size 22
647 —— Splendid uncirculated crown; 1679; letter C's interlocked between the angles of a cross. *Very rare.*
648 —— Shilling and sixpence; nearly as fine; same type.
2 p
649 —— Set of his Maundy money, by *Simon;* Uncirculated and beautiful. Rare. 4 p
650 JAMES II., 1685 to 1689; splendid uncirculated crown, 1688. Very rare.
651 —— Varieties of his gun money; 2 pieces uncirculated.
5 p
652 WILLIAM AND MARY, 1689 to 1685; half crown; extremely fine.
653 —— Coronation medal (in lead); William and Mary seated fronting, both holding wand and sceptre; the pattern and style of their dress, admirably displayed; rev. three figures standing; Dutch inscription; quaint; well preserved and interesting. Size 38
654 WILLIAM alone (to 1702); *extremely* fine crown; 1695. Rare.
655 —— Shilling and sixpence; uncirculated and brilliant. Rare. 2 p
656 —— Medal (in tin); 1695; bust; rev. NAMVR-ARX-ET CASTR-EXPVGN; (See Van Loon, iv. 200); uncirculated. Size 31
657 ANNA, 1702 to 1714; shilling (plain), and sixpence (plumes); brilliant. 2 p
658 —— Same; repeated. Very good. 2 p
659 —— Bronze medal; 1710; bust; rev. trophies, BETHV-NIA. FAND. ST. VENANTII. ET-ARIA-CAPTIS. Splendid proof. Size 30
660 —— Fine copper token, bearing a strong similitude to a farthing, and often mistaken for that little coin; a mistake that has been the cause of much sorrow.
661 GEORGE I., 1714 to 1727; guinea for Scotland, 1726; well preserved. Gold.

46   *Coins and Medals of Great Britain.*

662 SAME; shilling and sixpence for the South Sea Co. (S. S. C.); uncirculated and brilliant. Rare.   2 p
663 —— Shilling, with roses; uncirculated.
664 GEORGE II., 1727 to 1760; guinea, 1752. Fine.
665 —— Crown, 1743; uncirculated; roses. Rare.
666 —— Shillings as they left the die; young head, roses and plumes, 1736; and old head plain, 1758; brilliant. Rare.   2 p
667 —— Shilling and sixpence; brilliant.   2 p
668 —— Shillings of William, Anna, and George.   4 p
669 —— Sixpences; Anna and the Georges.   4 p
670 GEORGE III., 1760 to 1820; guinea; spade-shape shield; uncirculated. Scarce. Gold.
671 —— Crown; Pistrucci's die. Ordinary.
672 —— Pattern crown by Mills and T. Wyon; splendid proof. Rare.
673 —— Bank of England dollar; 1804; one fine. Scarce.   2 p
674 —— Half crown of 1816; new die; uncirculated. Scarce.   2 p
675 —— Same of 1819; proof. Rare.
676 —— Shilling of 1819; proof. Rare.
677 —— Sixpence of 1820; proof. Rare.
678 —— Shilling and sixpence of 1787. Brilliant.   2 p
679 —— Pattern sixpence, 1790; brilliant, proof. Rare.
680 —— Sixpence and shilling of 1787 and 1816; brilliant. 3 p
681 —— Coronation medal; silver.   Size 17
682 —— Shillings and other coins of the realm and colonies; counting 20 cts. sterling, the lot.
683 —— Half-pound piece, gold; 1817. *Fair.*
684 —— Ceylon Government; set of three pieces; brass, gilt; obv. CEYLON GOVERNMENT, and the denomination, (48, 96, 192, respectively); rev. elephant and date (1802); beautiful; strictly proof, and very rare.   3 p
685 GEORGE IV., 1820, 1830; Coronation medal, the dies and designs by Pistrucci; a proof impression, none the worse because covered by a steel-colored tarnish; rare. Silver.   Size 22
686 —— Same in bronze; beautiful proof.

Anglo-Saxon and English to Victoria. 47

687 GEORGE IV.; Crown, 1821, Pistrucci's dies; the edging in *raised* letters. Brilliant proof and very rare.
688 —— Half crown. Brilliant proof. Rare. —
689 —— Proof set; crown, half-crown, shilling, and sixpence; brilliant. Rare.
690 —— Half crown of 1825; rev. "Britannarum Rex;" proof. *Slight* scratch.
691 WILLIAM IV., 1830, 1837; Coronation medal; dies by W. Wyon; obv. bust of William; rev. bust of Adelaide; brilliant proof; the heads frosted; silver. Size 21. Rare.
691* —— Same in bronze. Splendid proof impression.
692 —— Half crown, shilling, and sixpence, 1834-5-6. Fine.
693 —— Sixpence, together with same of his predecessor and Victoria. All brilliant.
694 VICTORIA; crowned in 1837, sovereign gold. Uncirculated.
695 —— Her gothic crown, proof; but has by carelessness received a few slight scratches. Rare.
696 —— Uncirculated and brilliant set of her coins, from crown to penny; the set comprises the crown, half crown, florin, shilling, sixpence, ten cents, fourpence, threepence, twopence, and penny; ten pieces. Intrinsic value in silver $2.82.
697 —— Set comprising the half crown, rupee, florin, shilling, sixpence, fourpence, and threepence; all except half crown brilliant; seven pieces. Intrinsic value $1.90.
698 —— Same, except the half crown. All brilliant. 6 p
699 —— Same as last, except the rupee. 5 p
700 —— War medal for the Crimean campaign. Silver, poor.
701 —— Bronze medal, given as a prize in 1854; with Prince Albert's bust behind her own, by *Adams*. Beautiful proof. Size 40
702 —— Medal on her landing at Ostend in 1843, by Hart; beautiful work in the style called cavo-relievo; fine proof. Bronze. Size 34
703 SILVER coins of several reigns counting 13 shillings; the lot.

48   Coins and Medals of Great Britain.

ENGLISH MEDALS.
Bronze and Tin.

704 ALEXANDER POPE; by Dassier; bust; rev. POETA ANGLVS, 1741; bronze. Proof.   Size 44.
705 SAMUEL JOHNSON; by Smith; series numismatica.   Size 26
706 FRANCIS BACON and Roger Bacon. Same series.   2 p
707 JOHN LOCKE and Wm. Harvey. Same series.   2 p
708 REV. JOHN WESLEY; Centenary of Methodism, 1839; by Taylor. Tin proof.   Size 26
709 WALTER SCOTT; by W. Wyon; fine medal in bronze, and an impression from same dies in tin. Size 34. 2 p
710 BYRON; Greek medal; obv. bare head; his name in Greek letters, in the field to r.; rev. lightning issuing from clouds above; a group of laurel trees; Greek inscription below and on the edge; the artist's name does not appear, but it is one of the finest medals ever produced; equal to the Syracuse medallion for high relief and breadth of effect; fine proof. Bronze.   Size 40
711 WELLINGTON medal; by T. Wyon, 1821; obv. bust of the Duke; rev. Minerva and Mars. Bronze.   Size 32
712 MANCHESTER Riot medal, Aug. 16, 1819; troops cutting down the citizens; rev. quotation from the 37th psalm; in soft metal and bronzed. Very fine impression.   Size 40
713 FLORENCE NIGHTINGALE; obv. within an oval a half-length figure of F. N. with an open book; rev. within a circle of stars and palms a crown supported by a cross; the Queen's brave soldiers, etc.; by *Pinches*. Bronze.   Size 26
714 LORD NELSON; naked bust; rev. IPSE BELLI FULMEN. Bronze.   Size 32
715 WILLIAM PITT; R P Q B.; naked bust; rev. waves dashing against a rock, 1806. Bronze.   Size 32
716 FREDERICK, Duke of York; bust in the Roman style; rev. tomb. Tin.   Size 28
717 SIR ISAMBERT MARC BRUNEL; bust; rev. view of the Thames tunnel. Tin.   Size 38

English Copper Coins and Tokens. 49

718 FALL of Sebastopol, 1855; "The allies give peace to Europe, March 30, 1856." Bronze. Size 30
719 THE Thomason metallic vase; "begun," "completed," etc. View of the vase. Size 34
720 THE English army upon the Scheld, 1815; concord of the allies, Minden, 1759; and England gives a constitution to the Ionian islands; splendid medals by *Mudie;* bronze. Size 25. 3 p
721 THE battle of Toulouse; by same. Same size.
722 CRIMEAN war medals, recording brave actions at Alma, Balaklava, and Inkerman, by *Pingres;* splendid proofs; bronze. Size 25. 3 p
723 PRINCE of Wales, and other tin medals. 4 p

ENGLISH COPPER COINS AND TOKENS.

724 GEORGE III., 1797; uncirculated twopence, with the letters incused; slightly scratched; half stiver of Demarara, and farthing 1806. From uncirculated to proof. 3 p
725 —— Varieties of his coin. Fine to fair. 5 p
726 GEORGE IV.; uncirculated farthing from Pistrucci's dies, with penny, half-penny, and farthing. By Wyon. 4 p
727 WILLIAM IV.; uncirculated farthing (rare), and others, with some of George III. and IV. Fine to fair. 6 p
728 VICTORIA; uncirculated penny, half-penny, and farthing. 3 p
729 —— for New Brunswick, Nova Scotia, etc., with Canada of George III. and IV., and other Colonials. Fine lot. 15 p
730 MISCELLANEOUS English coins and tokens, and Sierra Leone, Bahama, Isle of Man, Canada, etc., etc. A very ordinary lot. 50 p
731 TRADESMEN's tokens, half-penny, and a few farthing size; in the lot, five varieties with Druid's head; three of Lady Godiva, Odd Fellows, Queen Bess, Daniel Eccleston, John Wilkes, Spence's, Pidcock's, etc. Uncirculated. 28 p
732 —— All half-penny size. Uncirculated. 30 p
733 —— Same. 50 p

4

COINS AND MEDALS OF FRANCE.

Gold and Silver Coins.

734 Louis XIV., 1643-1714; crown, 1711. Good; scarce.
735 Louis XV., 1715-1774; crown, young head, 1726. Good; scarce.
736 —— Crown, 1729.
737 —— Crown, old head, 1767. Good; scarce.
738 —— Silver jetons, value 1-3 crown each. Fine.   2 p
739 Louis XVI., 1774-1793; crown, 1785. Fine.
740 —— Crowns of 1785 and 1791. Good.   2 p
741 —— 30-sol., 1791 (1-3 crown); fine and scarce; with a jeton of Brittany; same size. Ex. fine.   2 p
742 —— Crown of 1792; rev. REGNE DE LA LOIS, and in ex., L'AN I DE LA LIBERTE. Ex. fine.
743 —— Duplicate. Equally fine.
744 Napoleon; First consul from 15th August, 1802, to 17th May, 1804, and Emperor from 1804, April 11th, 1814; 20-franc in gold; while he was Premier Consul. Uncirculated; by *Tioliér*. Rare.
745 —— 20 francs in gold, 1813; on this his head is laureated; dies by *Tioliér*. Equally fine; rare.
746 —— 5-francs of the Empire and Italy.   3 p
747 —— 2 and 1-francs.   3 p
748 Louis XVIII., 1814-1824; 5-francs, 1816. Good.
749 Charles X., 1824-1830; 5-francs, 1826. Good.
750 —— Same; 5-francs, 1828. Fine.
751 —— with his predecessors; value of 8-francs the lot.
752 Louis Philippe, 1830-1848; 5-francs, 1847, by *Domard*. Uncirculated; rare.
753 Republic of 1848; Hercules with Liberty and Fraternity, 1848 and 1849; 5-francs, each date.   2 p
754 —— Same of 1851; new dies; head of Ceres on the obverse. Uncirculated; scarce.
755 —— 20-francs; gold; 1849. Uncirculated; scarce.
756 Louis Napoleon; 10-francs and 5-francs, gold, 1856. Uncirculated.   2 p

Louis Napoleon ; Set silver coins, same date (1856) ; viz. :
5-francs, 2-francs, franc, and half-franc ; dies by *Barre*.
All ex. fine. 4 p
—— 5-francs, 1857, by *Bouvet*. Uncirculated ; rare.

French Medals.

With a single exception, bronze, and all fine proofs.

Louis XI., born 1423 ; old medal, with bust and ins. ; and another. Size 20. 2 p
Louis XIV. and Maria Theresa ; bust on each side ; fine medal by MAVGER. Size 26
Louis XVI. ; Prize medal, French Acad. ; by *Du Vivier*; struck in metal de cloche. Rare. Size 20
Lafayette ; military bust ; rev. IL A COMMANDE LA GARDE NATIONALE PARISIENNE EN 1789, 1790, ET 1791. Rare. Size 22
Napoleon as First Consul ; young bust, inscription surrounding it ; rev. same in nine parallel lines ; by *Brenet*. Size 32
—— Laureated bust ; rev. crown ; his coronation at Milan, 23d May, 1805 ; by Denon and Andrien. Size 24
—— Companion ; Orphans of the Army, etc.
Eugene Napoleon de Beauharnais ; by *Gayrard* ; bust in cloak and decoration ; rev. inscription, born, etc., etc. ; with wreath of laurel. Superb. Size 32
Joachim Napoleon Murat ; same size and style ; by *Cacqué*. Magnificent.
Camille Borghese ; same series, by *Rogat*. Equal to the others.
On the uprising in 1830 ; LIBERTE NATIONALE RECONQUISE PAR LE PEUPLE, 27, 28, 29, JUILLET ; head of Liberty, with axe and fasces ; rev. REGNE DES LOIS ; by *Pingret*. Size 24
On the same occasion ; double wreath, interlocked ; rev. lion guarding the French rooster. Size 24
On the same ; with revolutionary medal of 1848 ; Conquest of Egypt ; and another. 5 p

52   *Silver Coins of Spain and Mexico.*

772 MEDALS, with heads of ladies of Napoleon's family : Hortense, Eliza, Paulina, and Caroline ; done in the old Greek style, with Greek inscriptions. Extremely beautiful. Size 16. 4 p
773 —— One of the same series in silver. [These medals are done by various hands, as *Andrien, Denon,* etc.]
774 PRIZE medal by *Hart;* " The Province of Anvers to the Public Schools," 1840. Ex. fine work. Size 36
775 FRANCIS ARAGO, from his auditors during a course of astronomical discourses, with bare bust of Arago.
Size 36
776 VICTOR HUGO ; plain bust, without reverse. Size 32
777 NAPOLEON III. ; on the taking of Sebastopol, 1855 ; by *Borrel.* Size 26
778 —— On his coronation. Size 32
779 —— On his election in 1852. Size 20
780 —— With Eugenie ; their busts accolated ; on the occasion of the birth of the Prince ; by *Montagny.*
Size 32
781 —— Another ; bust on each side. Size 30

COPPER COINS OF FRANCE.

782 MONNERON FRERES, Cinq Sols, Louis Philippe. Charles X., Republican coins, etc. Selected, and all fine. 10 p
783 MISCELLANEOUS. 50 p

SILVER COINS OF SPAIN AND MEXICO.

784 COB half-dollar, old pillar half-dollar, same from Mexican mint, and a proclamation half-dollar of Habana, 1834 ; the latter fine proof and rare. 4 p
785 COB and other quarter-dollars of Barcelona (siege), Joseph Napoleon, Proclamation, Pistareens, etc. 10 p
786 EIGHTS and 16ths (reals and half-reals), including one of Iturbide, Emperor of Mexico, which is rare. (6 reals and 4 half-reals.) 10 p
787 DOLLAR (30-sol.) of Catalonia ; a piece of necessity of Ferd. VII., 1808. Uncirculated ; rare.

Coins of Portugal, Brazil, Etc. 53

788 DOLLAR (5-pesetas) of Barcelona, 1810; also a siege dollar; arms of Barcelona within a broad wreath. Ex. fine; rare.
789 —— Same of Ferd. VII., from Mexican mint, 1816. Fine.
790 —— Same of Ferd. VI., Charles IIII., and one which went to China and came home punched. Fine lot.
    3 p
791 —— Same of Ferd. VI., Maximilian, Emperor of Mexico, and the Rep. of 1861. From very fine to uncirculated.   5 p
792 SET from dollar to 16th (5 pieces, ex. fine) of Isabella, 1851; really beautiful, and now difficult to collect; $1.94 intrinsic value the set.
793 —— Repetition, without the dollar. 4 pieces the lot.
794 —— Same.
795 MAXIMILIAN, Emperor. Fine dollar.
796 MEXICAN dollar, half-dollar, and set of Isabella's coins—same as 794. Intrinsic value, $2.44 the lot.

COINS OF PORTUGAL, BRAZIL,

AND OTHER S. A. STATES AND THE REPUBLIC OF HAYTI.

797 PORTUGAL; "Half-Joe" (eight dollars) of John V., 1745; gold.
798 —— Double Joe (thirty-two dollars), or 20,000 Reis of same, 1726. Extremely fine; gold; rare.
799 —— Dollar and half-dollar, 1810. Very fine.   2 p
800 BRAZIL; Petrus II.; dollar, half, and quarter,-1856. Uncirculated.   3 p
801 —— Half-dollar; duplicate.   2 p
802 COPPER Coins belonging to Portugal or Brazil, or both (nothing but infinite wisdom can separate them)—presenting a broad and fine appearance, some thick, some thin; sometimes with the figures 40 displayed on a thin piece, again, with 20 decorating one much thicker. Altogether a fine and characteristic lot, apparently uncirculated.   15 p

54 *Coins of Portugal, Brazil, Etc.*

803 NEW GRANADA; Un Peso; Bogota Mint, 1857; beautiful uncirculated dollar. Scarce.
804 ECUADOR; two reals, coined in 1840 at Quito. Scarce.
805 VENEZUELA; Cob quarters of Caracus. Very fine. 2 p
806 COLOMBIA; Dollar of 1821; Indian head; rev. ripe fruit, S, 8 R. Finer than usually found.
807 PERU; dollar of 1834; (Liberty standing). Very fine.
808 —— Same of 1837; coined at Cuzco, South Peru; obv. sun and 4 stars; rev. volcano and castle. Ex. fine.
809 —— Duplicate of last. Equally fine.
810 —— Dollar and half-dollar, (sol, and half-sol); coined at Lima, 1867. Ex. fine; nearly uncirculated. 2 p
811 BOLIVIA; dollar of 1838; bust of Simon Boliva in military dress, with his name below; rev. two llamas lying down under a tree. Extra fine; rare.
812 —— Same; laureated head; same; rev. 1846. Equally fine dollar.
813 —— Half-dollar; brilliant. Uncirculated; rare.
814 LA PLATA; or, Argentine Confederacy; two reals, 1813; and another. Scarce; fair. 2 p
815 CHILI; dollar (Un Peso) of Santiago, 1817; volcano in action; rev. globe on a high column under a star; LIBERTAD on a schedule. Fine and scarce.
816 —— Dollar and half-dollar of 1853; Condor. 2 p
817 HAYTI (W. I.); President Boyer's Currency dollar, half, and quarter-dollar. Poor. 3 p
818 —— Beautiful, and in this condition *rare*, set of 50c., 25c., 12c., and 6c. 4 p
819 GUIANA; Provisional copper money; not common. Fine lot. 6 p
820 DUPLICATES of small silver coins coming under this head; with a few others. All of a good quality of silver; intrinsic value, $3.00 as one lot.
821 ACCLAMATION of the miners of Guanajuato on the accession of Carolus IIII., Oct. 28, 1790. Fine gilt medal, and counterfeit dollar of Mexico. 2 p
822 UNCOMMON copper coins of Spain and Mexico. Some rare. 12 p

COINS OF ITALY.

823 ANCONA; double denarius; St. SOVIRIACVS standing; rev. cross DE ANCONA; and pennies of similar character. Fine and rare. 6 p
824 GENOA; broad and fine crown of the Republic, dated 1692. Hardly circulated.
825 TUSCANY; Ferd. II., Grand Duke, 1620; with several of Florence, Venice, and Rome; all English groat size, and about 16th century. Fine and rare lot. 8 p
826 —— Charles Louis, and Eliza; their busts, the latter diademed; rev. coat-of-arms on a shield, the points of a cross, which is behind, showing at the sides. Uncirculated double thaler, 1805.
827 —— Duplicate. Equally fine.
828 —— Crown of same, 1806; on this their busts vis-a-vis. Very fine.
829 —— Duplicate. Equally fine.
830 —— Crowns of Leopold, Louis I., and Leopold II. Fine and very fine. 3 p
831 —— Splendid uncirculated crown of Leopold II., 1856.
832 —— Quarter-dollar and 10 quattrini of same. Uncirculated. 2 p
833 —— Thalers and quarters (2ths and 4qrs). 6 p
834 SARDINIA; Charles Felix; 5 lire, 1827. Very fine.
835 —— Same 1828. Very fine.
836 —— Charles Albert, 1837; same. Very fine.
837 —— Victor Emmanuel II.; same, 1851. Very fine.
838 LUCCA; St. Martin dollar, 1743. Ex. fine; rare.
839 —— Duplicate. Very fine.
840 SUB-ALPINE Gaul; 5 francs, L'AN-IO. Very fine.
840* VENICE; Republic of 1848; *Gold* 20 LIRE. Very fine and rare.
841 —— Republic of 1848; 5 Lire. Uncirculated. 2 p
842 —— Old coin, about half size of last, 1757.
843 NAPLES; Joachim Murat, King of the two Sicilies; 5 Lire, 1813. Extremely fine; barely circulated; rare.
844 SICILY; Scudo, 1734; 120 Granas. Good.

Coins of Italy.

845 SICILY Ducato; 100 granas (dollar size), of Ferdinand IV., 1785. Fine.
846 —— Same. 2 p
847 —— Same, 50 granas, and another. 2 p
848 —— Ferd. II., 1858. Brilliant uncirculated dollar and half-dollar (120 and 60 granas). 2 p
849 ROMAN Republic of 1798; obv. standing figure of Liberty, REPVBLICA ROMANA; rev. within a heavy wreath, SCVDO ROMANO; very broad milling; dies by *Mercandetti*. Extra fine and rare dollar (See Wellenheim 4,890).
849* —— Republic of 1848; 40 Baiocchi. A beautiful uncirculated coin, and rare.
850 —— Same; 16 Baiocchi. Equally fine.
851 COSMUS III., Grand Duke Etruria, 1670, 1723; obv. bust; rev. baptism, FILIVS MEVS DILECTVS, 1681; medal crown. Superb. Size 28

[This rare crown was omitted by oversight from its place among the coins of Tuscany, as was also the one following].

852 LEOPOLD II., 1832; gold ducat, lily; rev. John Babtist. Very fine.
853 FERDINAND II., 1852; six ducati (gold coin, about 6 dolls.), bust; rev. angel standing by a column supporting a crown, in one hand shield charged with three fleur de lis. Nearly uncirculated.
854 —— Same; 3 ducati. Equally fine.

[Last two omitted under coins of Sicily by mistake.]

855 FLORENCE (?); Gold ducat, without date, and one 1786; on one St. Peter, the other St. John; on each a flower, rose and lily. Very fine. 2 p
856 —— Floreno of Leopold II., Grand Duke, Tuscany, bust; rev. Lily, 1828 (quarter dollar). Fine. 2 p
857 UNCIRCULATED Coins of Sicily and Roman Republic of 1848 (a beautiful series of Ferdinand II.) in copper; with silver coins of small intrinsic value, but almost impossible to obtain in this condition. 12 p

Miscellaneous Foreign Coins. 57

COINS OF DENMARK, NORWAY, AND SWEDEN.

858 CHRISTIAN VII., for Schleswig-Holstein, 1794; full dollar Fine.
859 FREDERIC VI.; Rigs bank dollar, 1813. Scarce.
860 —— Same of 1835. Very fine.
861 CHRISTIAN VIII., 1846; beautiful uncirculated "Species" dollar; fine rev. Scarce.
862 OSCAR, 1848; Rigs species dollar; handsome rev. Very fine.
863 —— Same of 1856. Ex. fine.

MISCELLANEOUS FOREIGN COINS.

864 MARIA Therese; dollar, 1780. Uncirculated.
865 —— Duplicate. Ordinary.
866 LOVE thaler of Frankfort; double thaler by Nordheim. Beautiful; scarce.
867 WILLIAM, King of Brunswick and Lun.; double thaler of 1856. Ex. fine.
868 NUREMBERG; dollar, 1786; view of the city. Very fine.
869 MAX JOSEPH, Bavaria, 1809; broad dollar. Fair.
870 OLD Dutch Patagon, 1641; rude work; well preserved. Now rare.
871 OLD Daler of Zeland, 1679; "Luctor Et Emergo."
872 PISA, crown of Francis, Duke 1765. Rare and in fair condition.
873 BADEN, Leopold, Grand Duke, 1848; uncirculated dollar.
874 ERNEST AUGUSTUS, King of Hanover, 1846; thaler.
875 LEOPOLD, Belgium, King in 1856; 5 francs. Fine.
876 POLAND, the last king, Augustus; ¼ thaler, with several uncommon coins, av. same size. 32 p
877 FREDERICK, King of Brunswick and Lunenburg in 1646; Broad crown of that date. Fine and rare.
878 LEOPOLD I., Germany; crown of 1660; pierced.
879 FERD. III., do ducat, 1652; gold. Rare.
880 BELGIUM; uncirculated ducats (gold) of 1841. Beautiful.
2 p

Oriental Coins.

881 RUSSIA and Helvetia; set of silver coins of each; av. value about 15 cts. each. 5 p
882 MODERN Greece; 5 francs of Otho, King 1833.
883 AUSTRIA; duadruple ducat (gold) of Francis II., 1793. Fine.
884 —— Double ducat (gold) of Francis I., 1835. Fine.
885 —— Ducat (gold) Francis Joseph, 1857; uncirculated.
886 —— Half-thaler, same; uncirculated.
887 PRUSSIA; Frederick the Great thaler, 1750 and 1786; 2 varieties. Ordinary. 2 p
888 —— Frederick William IV., 1859, double thaler; uncirculated.
889 —— Various thalers; all circulated. 7 p
890 SAXONY, thalers, 1830 and 1845. 2 p
891 SILVER coins of Germany and Italy, from gulden to 5-kreutzer size; difficult to estimate, but certainly of the average value of 10 cts. each: 50 p
892 SMALL base coins. 20 p
893 OLD baronial coins, coppers of the German cities and corporations, pennies, etc. A fine lot.
894 —— Similar, but inferior lot. 38 p

ORIENTAL COINS.

895 GOLD Beshlik and onlik, and other small thin coins. 4 p
896 FINE gold coin of Turkey; about $2.
897 COBANG of Japan, gold (5 or 6 dols.); uncertain value.
898 DOLLAR of Turkey; good silver, full value. Very fine.
899 —— Duplicate. Equally fine.
900 —— Slightly debased, and half same. 2 p
901 SMALL Turkish coins of fine silver; av. value 6 cts. 8 p
902 BASE silver of Turkey; fine lot of large coins, all with the Sultan's monogram (Toghra), but bearing marks of different countries. Old. 9 p
903 MISCELLANEOUS base coins of caliphs, and the Turk; among them, thick copper coins. 16 p
904 CASH (Chinese). 16 p

Papal Medals and Coins.

905 BACTRIAN coin; very old; on one side a horseman riding to l., on the other the sacred bull of the Brahmins lying down; Cufic ins. A fine silver coin (didrachm), and very rare.

906 —— A still more barbarous and equally remarkable and valuable coin, on each side a crowned head of the rudest possible execution, with characters which I suppose are Cufic; silver. Size 16

907 SILVER coins of the Moguls; wholly different from the ordinary India rupees. 8 p

908 OLD rupees; one with Cufic inscription, the other with ins. in the Assamese character on one side; rev. a picture of two wild cats, each supporting a banner with a strange device. Both very fine and rare coins. 2 p

909 RUPEE, half and quarter, do. 3 p

910 HALF and quarter rupees. 4 p

PAPAL MEDALS AND COINS.

[It would be tedious to measure and repeat the size of each of this long series of medals. I shall therefore say here that they are of the average breadth of the old crowns, though much thicker, especially in the centre. The oldest are cast, many of the later are from dies by such artists as *Girometti* and *Hamerani*. They are all strictly fine, which may also as well be stated here, and omitted in the descriptions, and bronze unless some more valuable metal is mentioned.]

911 ANICETUS, A.D. 168; Eugenius II., 824. 2 p

912 BENEDICT VIII., 1024 (said to have been seen on a black horse after his death); Sylvester III., 1045. 2 p

913 DAMASUS II., 1047; Innocent VII., 1404. 2 p

914 EUGENIUS II., A.D. 1153; Martin V., 1431 (he condemned Wycliffe, and burned John Huss and Jerome of Prague). 2 p

915 NICOLAUS V., 1455 (he built the Vatican); Calistus III., 1458. 2 p

916 PIUS II., 1464; Paul II., 1471 (he enriched his mitre with gems, and introduced the use of scarlet gowns). 3 p

917 SIXTUS IV., 1484 (he founded the Vatican Library and brought in books); Innocent VIII., 1492. 2 p
918 ALEXANDER VI., 1503; Pius III.; same as last (sat only 25 days). 2 p
919 JULIUS II., 1513 (one, splendid, from dies by *Carbara*). 3 p
920 LEO X., 1522 (burned Luther's books; was a liberal patron of the arts). Very fine. 2 p
921 ADRIAN VI., 1523; Clement VII., 1524 (he quarreled with Henry VIII. of England). 3 p
922 PAUL III., 1549 (called the Council of Trent); Julius III. 1555. Extra fine, no duplicate. 4 p
923 PAUL IV., 1569; rev. bust of Christ, with a half-scudo (silver coin). Rare. 2 p
924 MARCELLUS II., 1555; Pius V., 1572. Very fine. 2 p
925 GREGORY XIII. 1585 (changed the Calendar to the new style; was charged with favoring the massacre at Paris). Very fine. 2 p
926 SIXTUS V., 1590 (one by *Bonis*, very fine). 3 p
927 URBAN VII., 1590; Gregory XIV., 1591, with Innocent IX. All beautiful proofs, *Bonis*. 3 p
928 CLEMENT VIII., 1604; Paul V., 1621. 2 p
929 PAUL V.; testoon dated 1615; rev. St. Paul standing (He was charged with promoting the Gunpowder Plot). Fine and rare. 2 p
930 GREGORY XV., 1623; Urban VIII., 1644. 4 p
931 URBAN VIII. again; no duplicates. 3 p
932 LEO XI. (28 days), and Innocent X. to 1655. 3 p
933 ALEXANDER VII., 1667. By *G. M.* Very fine. 4 p
[On one, fine view of St. Peter's.]

934 —— Scudo, shield; above St. Peter; rev. St. Thomas giving alms to a beggar (see Madai 671; Well. 4194). Rare and fine.
935 CLEMENT IX., 1669 (on a reverse of one of these we see from whence came the design of the Gen. Taylor "Pelican" medal). Die by *Amerano*. All very fine. 3 p
936 CLEMENT X., 1675; Innocent XI., 1689. 3 p

Papal Medals and Coins. 61

937 INNOCENT XI. (one, DIVINE NVNCIA MENTIS). 2 p
938 —— Half-scudo of his last year, 1689. Very fine and rare.
939 ALEXANDER VIII., 1691; splendid medal. Size 40
940 —— Half-scudo, 1690; rev. yoke of oxen. Very fine, pierced, rare.
941 —— Same and testoon. 2 p
942 INNOCENT XII., 1700. By *Hameranus*. Splendid medals, not duplicates. 2 p
943 —— Testoon, 1697. Very fine.
944 CLEMENT XI., 1721; splendid; by *Hameranus*; rev. Christ bearing the Cross Size 33
945 —— Same, and another. Same hand. 2 p
946 —— Half scudo; no date; uncirculated and brilliant. Size 23
947 INNOCENT XIII., 1724; by *Hamerani*; splendid, with half scudo of Clement XI. 2 p
948 BENEDICT XIII., 1730; with one of Innocent XIII. 2 p
949 BENEDICT XIV., 1758; by *Cropanese*, and half scudo. 2 p
950 —— By *Hamerani*; medal and testoon. 2 p
951 —— Same; with one testoon. Silver. 2 p
952 CLEMENS XIII., 1769; gold coin, 1758; Ducat. Fine and rare.
953 —— By *Cropanese*; two bronze, and one in lead. 3 p
954 SEDE VACANTE, 1781; fine crown (ten marks); City of Eystett. Bird's eye view of the city.
955 PIUS VI., 1799; fine scudo, 1780, and another 1795. 2 p
956 —— Half scudi. 2 p
957 —— Silver coins, two and three pauls each; intrinsic value of the lot $2.00. Six pieces as one lot.
958 —— Extremely fine and rare set base silver coins uncirculated, viz.: Two carleni, 5 baiocchi, eight do. and four do. 6 p
959 —— Medal, 1778, and thick copper coins. 4 p
960 PIUS VII., 1823; five scudi or two ducats. Gold.
961 —— Silver medal; by *Cerbara* (2 oz.); obv. crowned bust of Pius Septimus in his robes; rev. Interior of the NOVVM MVSEVM, etc. Size 26

62   *Papal Medals and Coins.*

961* PIUS VII.; Scudi; lettered edge and milled do. The last by *Hamerani*. Both very fine, 1802 and 1816.   2 p
962 —— Medals, by *Mercandetti* and *Pasinati* (one reverse of the antique statue of the Laocooon). Very fine.   2 p
963 —— Medal and silver coin (about forty cts.)   2 p
964 LEO XII., 1829; splendid medal, by *Nic. Cerbara*; obv. bust; rev. Christ standing beside his Cross; on each side a group of standing and sitting figures representing Justice, Fortune, and several of the muses. Extra fine.   Size 36
965 —— Fine medal; by *Girometti*, and two small do. 3 p
966 PIUS VIII., 1830; medals by *Girometti* and *Carbara*.   2 p
967 —— Thirty baiocchi. Fine.
968 SEDE VACANTE, 1830, medals (not duplicates).   3 p
969 GREGORY XVI.; scudo, 1834.
970 —— Bust in cap and mantle, trimmed with fur; rev. angel descending, attended by cherubs; the Pope kneeling in front of a temple; his crown on the pavement. Superb medal by *Girometti*.   Size 38
971 —— Companion; by same hand.
972 —— Obv.; the Pope's bust as before within thick wreath of laurel and oak; rev. interior of the Egyptian museum, founded by Gregory; equally splendid work and impression by same.   Size 32
973 —— Companion.
974 —— Large and small medals.   3 p
975 PIUS IX., now Pope; gold 2½, scudo. Uncirculated.
976 —— Scudo. Gold. Uncirculated.
977 —— Silver medal; large and splendid, by *Cerbara*; obv. bust of Pius IX., cap and mantle; rev. bust of Raphael Sanchus Urbino. Very thick.   Size 38
978 —— Same; by *Girometti*; rev. Christ blessing little children; beautiful proof. Silver.   Size 28
979 —— Same; rev. interior of the museum in the Lateran Palace. Same series.
980 —— Prize college medal. Silver, and uncirculated.
981 —— Scudi, 1854. Uncirculated.   2 p

Bronze Medals.

982 Pius IX., now Pope; Bronze medals; by *Cerbara* and *Girometti*. 2 p

983 —— Medal; by *Zacagnine;* view of the Colliseum; one by *Girometti*—Casines Mediccs; and by same, of *Francis Guiciardini;* splendid proofs. Size 26. 3 p

984 Papal silver coins, counting $2½, the lot.

985 —— Copper coins. 20 p

986 Old Roman and other medals (not papal.) 10 p

987 Cast and repousse medals; one in lead of Francis Foscarius. *Rare* lot.

988 Silver medal, Religious, 1697. Size 19

989 Dante, Allighieri; splendid medal by *Sutinatti*, Feb. 11, 1835; bust; rev. Rome seated; by her side a shield with the Papal arms; in her hand an open book, with a plain inscription, SANTE SEDE CHIESA, 1799; fine proof. Silver. Size 30

990 Louis XVIII. and the Duchess D'Angoleme, on two oval placques; Frederick the Great at the battle of Rosbach; "Souvenir Immortel" of Napoleon, and five others. 9 p

991 Coin weights, tokens, and Roman coins. Extra fine. 12 p

992 Jetons, tokens, and Roman coins. 50 p

993 Russian copper coins. 12 p

994 —— For Siberia, large copper of ten kopecs under Elizabeth; Petrovna (the only coinage), 1776; obv. within a wreath of laurel and palm, her cypher crowned; rev. shield and crown supported by two Arctic foxes. Extra fine. Size 30

995 —— Same. Five kopecs. Size 24

996 Bag of miscellaneous copper coins. 400 p

BRONZE MEDALS.

997 Christopher Columbus, bust; rev. GENOVA, 1846. Fine medal, by *Girometti*. Size 36

998 Dante, bust; rev. inscription; by *Cerbara*. Size 26

999 —— Same, by *Gayrard*. Series Numismatica.

1000 Cervantes; by same. Same series.

Bronze Medals.

1001 JOHN CALVIN; by same. Same series.

1002 SCHILLER; by *Barre*. Same series.

1003 CICERO; by *Vivier*. Same series.

1004 CHRISTINA (Regina); by *Travanus;* a cast medal with Greek inscription on rev., 1665; obv. helmeted head; rev. Phœnix. Size 38

1005 —— Same; laureated bust, draped in the Roman manner; rev. MI NIHII IN TER RIS.; also a cast medal. Both original and rare. Size 38

1006 PETER THE GREAT, 1703; laureated bust in military habit; rev. two ships with a large number of boats filled with soldiers. Fine proof in light red bronze. Size 34

1007 CATHERINE II.; companion medal.

1008 CORREGIO, bust; rev. Christ ascending; from a painting by himself in the Vatican. Superb medal by *Cerbara*. Size 38

1009 VICTORIA COLUMNA; laureated bust; Roman; rev. Phœnix within heavy wreath, ALEXANDER TORLONIA THERESIAE COLVNINAE VXORIS SVAE GRATIA REST*. Splendid, by *Girometti*. Size 38

1010 MEDAL to commemorate the restoration of an edifice by Gregory XVI.; rev. front of a cathedral; rev. inscription. Extra fine. Size 36

1011 MEHEMET ALI; bust; rev. sword upright; inscription in Turkish and French; Fine proof, by *Rogat*, 1840. Size 32

1012 COMMEMORATIVE medal in honor of Metastasio, Visconti, and Pinnellio; medallion busts of the three illustrious men; by *Girometti*, Rome 1840. Fine and rare. Size 32

1013 THORWALDSEN. Fine medal of *Brandt*. Size 23

1014 CANOVA; by *Putinati;* rev. cap of Mercury and head of Pallas, within snake ring. Size 32

1015 PRIZE and another bronze medal. 2p

PART II.

AMERICAN.

Colonial and State Coins and Tokens.

1652.

1016 Pine Tree shilling; very broad planchet; large letters; limbs of the tree upright. *Extremely* fine.

1017 Oak Tree shilling; also broad and fine; good match to last.

1018 Pine Tree three-pence; limbs at right angles. *Extra* fine.

1019 Pine Tree two-pence; equally fine; in this condition very rare.

1020 —— Duplicate three-pence. Ordinary.

1694.

1021 Carolina; elephant half-penny; elephant; rev. GOD PRESERVE CAROLINA AND THE LORD'S PROPRIETORS, 1694; not absolutely *fine*, but a very good and desirable example of this rare and valuable cent.

1721 to 1723.

1022 Louisiana cent; COLONIES FRANCOISES, 1721.

1023 Same, 1722; both unusually sharp and fine.

1024 Rosa-Americana; two-pence, 1722; plain rose; good impression; well preserved, but dark.

1025 Same; penny (half-penny size); same date, variety, and condition.

1026 Same; half-penny (farthing size); same.

1027 Same; penny, 1723; rose crowned, very fine; no marks of circulation, and good color. Rare.

66   *American.*

1766 and 1767.

1028 PITT Token, 1776; NO STAMPS; very good, dark.
1029 LOUISIANA cent, 1767; two sceptres crossed; R. F. counterstamped on rev. Very fine.
1030 SAME; without counterstamp.

1773 and 1776.

1031 VIRGINIA cent, 1773; usual type; large planchet. Very fine.
1032 CONTINENTAL currency, 1776; I. W. counterstamped on one side; tin. Original.

1783.

1033 GEORGIUS TRIUMPHE cent. Very good.
1034 NOVA CONSTELLATIO; U. S., in capitals and script. Very good.   2 p
1035 UNITY States cent, 1783; "Washington and Independence." Very fine.
1036 WASHINGTON and Independence; rev. United States; one with two heads; two varieties of the former. 3 p
1037 SAME; bright proof impressions; edge milled; restruck from original dies.

1785 to 1788.

1038 NOVA CAESAREA (New Jersey); cent, 1786. Fine and rare.
1039 SAME; no two alike, 1787; good example.   5 p
1040 SAME; M. M.; small animal (dog or fox); 1788 struck over another coin; not fine, but rare and desirable for variety.
1041 CONNECTICUT cents, 1785, 1786, 1787, and 1788; interesting varieties embracing nearly all the *types*. In ordinary condition.   17 p
1042 MASSACHUSETTS cent, 1787. Very good example.
1043 —— Half-cent to match. Finer.
1044 SAME; cent, 1788; with half cent; same date. Very good pair.   2 p

Colonial and State Coins and Tokens. 67

1045 VERMONT cent; laureated head to r.; 1787 and 1788; as good as usually found, and scarce. 2 p
1046 SAME; landscape at sunrise over a plough, 1786; fine for type. Rare.
1047 FRANKLIN, cents, 1787; uncirculated; one an original impression. 2 p
1048 IMMUNE COLUMBIA, 1785; Columbia sitting on a square seat, which two years later the sanguine artist changed to a *globe* (not always "Fortune's wheel" even to the Goddess of Liberty); rev. NOVA CONSTELLATIO; very fine, nearly uncirculated, and extremely rare.

> [There is a dash of poetry about the early National coins, and this is one of the finest of them; compare any of them with our present coins; to be sure we have adopted Cromwell's motto, "Trust in God (and keep your powder dry)," but has the nation to-day a genius equal to Thomas Simon ?]

1049 IMMUNIS COLUMBIA; Columbia seated on a globe, 1787; rev. eagle displayed, E PLURIBUS UNUM; extremely fine impression, showing no marks of circulation, except on points of the highest relief; in this condition, rare.
1050 EXCELSIOR cent, 1787; obv. Arms of New York; rev. similar to last; as fine as last, and the same degree of rarity.
1051 GEORGE CLINTON cent; obv. bust; rev. EXCELSIOR; Arms of New York; a well-preserved and desirable example of one of the rarest of our State coins, 1787.
1052 NOVA EBORAC, 1787; rev. Liberty seated to r. Fair.
1053 CONFEDERATIO; rev. "Americana Inimica Tyrannis," 1785; fine. From Mr. Bolen's dies.

1791.

1054 WASHINGTON cent; bust; rev. large eagle; very fine, but little circulated. Rare.

1792.

1055 WASHINGTON cent; undraped bust to r. head laureated; below, 1792; rev. eagle displayed, six stars around his head; above CENT; edge lettered; circulated and abused before its value was known; still a fair cent, and one with which any collector would be satisfied unless his ambition led him to aspire to one of the 5 proofs of this rarest of American copper coins.

1056 SAME; bust to l. in military dress; date below; G. WASHINGTON, PRESIDENT; rev. eagle, around his head 15 stars; UNITED STATES OF AMERICA; edge plain; half-dollar size; impressions for silver from same dies are called half dollars; very fine; among the best ever offered, although not strictly uncirculated. Very rare.

1794 and 1795.

1057 WASHINGTON Grate cent; bust; rev. fire-place; London, 1795. Very fine.

1057* TALBOT ALLUM AND LEE; cents of each date, (1794–5); the last uncirculated and bright. Both fine. 2 p

1796.

1058 KENTUCKY; P. P. P. Myddelton's Token; "British Settlement in Kentucky;" illustrated by Liberty standing with outstretched hand before a woman and two children; anchor and other symbols lying on the ground; rev. Britannia seated; splendid proof, silver. Very rare.

1059 —— Same, "Unanimity is the strength of Society," "Our cause is just." Lettered edge, very fine.

1060 —— Same; edge plain. Equally fine, rare.

1060* PATTERN cent, without date, U. S. A.; rev. 13 bars. Extra fine.

UNITED STATES COINS, FROM THE ESTABLISHMENT OF THE MINT TO 1875.

1793.

1061 CENT; rev. a chain of 15 links, UNITED STATES OF AMERI; after the word Liberty no dot; unusually fine for date and variety. Very rare.

United States Coins.

CENT; rev. chain; the legend UNITED STATES OF AMERICA; dot after Liberty; sharp, fine impression, but little worn, but dark. Rare.
—— Same; rev. wreath; leaves of the trefoil broad, and standing fairly under the head; very sharp impression, and but little circulated, but with nicks on edge, and has been cleaned.
—— Same; another variety of the "wreath" cent; letters and figures on obv. smaller than before, the trefoil inclined to r., leaves slender. Very fine.
—— Same, with Liberty cap, lettered edge. A fine cent, *cleaned*, rare.
HALF-CENT; usual, and only type, fine. Rare.
—— Same; uncirculated; a beautiful impression, second to none ever offered at public or private sale. Very rare.

1794.

CENT; only fair; dark.
—— Same; very fine, broken die; also dark.
HALF-CENT; fair.
HALF-DIME; very fine, not uncirculated. Rare.
DOLLAR; fine for this rare date.
—— Same; the best impression from the dollar dies of this date, and on the best planchet that I have seen —a remark that I have often heard from others since the piece has been in my hands; there has been a name engraved on the obv. and burnished out, the effect being observable though not greatly hurtful; it is a beautiful dollar, and equalled by few. Rare.

1795.

CENT; lettered edge, thick planchet; dark, but fine. Scarce.
—— Same; plain edge; uncirculated, or very nearly so; impression and color all that can be desired. Rare.
—— Same; very rare variety, very broad milling. Fair.
—— Same; Jefferson head; the second best that has been offered at auction. Desirable and rare.

1078 HALF-CENT; lettered edge, thick planchet. Very fine
1079 —— Same; plain edge. Only fair.
1080 —— Same; lettered edge, thick planchet, bright and uncirculated; as fine in every respect as when it fell from the die; was to my knowledge sold two years ago for $35. Very rare.
1081 HALF-DIME; very fine. Scarce.
1082 HALF-DOLLAR; fine for date; considerably circulated.
1083 DOLLAR; flowing hair. Very fine, nearly uncirculated.
1084 —— Same; fillet head. Fine, very scarce.

1796.

1085 CENT; head with Liberty cap. Fine, rare.
1086 —— Same; fillet head; bright and uncirculated. Rare.
1087 —— Same; variety of same type. Ordinary.
1088 HALF-CENT, in good and satisfactory condition for the piece. A fair impression, and very rare.
1088* HALF-DIME; fine for date, but considerably circulated.
1089 DIME; very fine, almost uncirculated. Rare.
1090 —— Same; fine, not equal to last. Rare.
1091 QUARTER-DOLLAR. *Very* fine, rare.
1092 —— Same. Ordinary.
1093 HALF-DOLLAR; *very fine for date.* Very rare.
1094 DOLLAR; unusually fine for date. Scarce.

1797.

1095 CENT; very sharp impression, dark.
1096 —— Same; one of the uncirculated red cents of this date, so well known, but not one of the finest of the kind, still very desirable. Now rare.
1097 HALF-CENT; very good. Scarce.
1098 HALF-DIME; good for date.
1099 DIME; fine for date. Rare.
1100 —— Same; another. Fair.
1101 HALF-DOLLAR; fine for date, and very rare.
1102 DOLLAR; *six* and ten stars. Very fine for variety.
1103 —— Same; *seven* and nine stars. Still finer and scarce.

1798.

1104 CENT; sharp and fine, but dark.
1105 DIME; 13 stars on obv. and 16 on rev. Very fine for date and variety, rare.
1106 DOLLAR; old or *small* eagle reverse, and one of the best that I have seen. *Fine* and rare.
1107 —— Same; large eagle reverse; new die. Very fine.
1108 DUPLICATE ; equally fine.

1799.

1109 CENT; excellent impression and preservation; found nearly black and kept so; has not been cleaned, and is the better for it; a *very* desirable cent. Rare.
1110 DOLLAR. Very fine.
1111 —— Same, with *five* stars before the head and eight behind it; uncommonly fine for variety. Rare.

1800.

1112 CENT; broken die. Very good, dark.
1113 HALF-CENT. Very good.
1114 HALF-DIME. Very good, scarce.
1115 DIME. Ordinary.
1116 DOLLAR ; good for date.

1801.

1117 CENT ; broken die ; uncommonly fine, but dark.
1118 —— Same; on reverse $\overset{1}{\underset{000}{}}$; a rare variety. Good. 2 p
1119 HALF-DIME ; good for date. Scarce.
1120 DIME; ordinary. Scarce.
1121 DOLLAR; uncirculated and brilliant; no other known in this condition, consequently in the condition described, unique.
1122 —— Same. Very fine.

1802.

1123 CENT. Very fine, dark.
1124 —— Same ; very fair ; nearly uncirculated ; has been cleaned.
1125 HALF-CENT; much better than usually found. Rare.

1126 HALF-DIME; has been considerably circulated in a bent form, and worn in ridges; the date is, however, perfect, as well as other parts of the piece on both sides. I am told that it was formerly in the Sandford Collection, and sold with his coins. Rare to excess.
1127 DIME; ordinary.
1128 HALF-DOLLAR; for date excellent. Rare.
1129 DOLLAR; fine for date.

1803.

1130 CENT, uncirculated, but with slight drawbacks; the color is not all that could be desired, and there are scratches on the face. Rare.
1131 —— Same; dark, rather ordinary.
1132 HALF-CENT; ordinary.
1133 HALF-DIME; good for date. Scarce.
1134 DIME; better; *fine* for date. Scarce.
1135 HALF-DOLLAR; *fine*.
1136 DOLLAR; *fine*.

1804.

1137 CENT; broken die; fine for date. Rare.
1138 HALF-CENTS; very fine. 2 p
1139 DIME. Much worn and scratched, but very rare.
1140 QUARTER-DOLLAR. Ordinary; scarce.

1805.

1141 CENT; uncirculated, strictly; much original color remaining. Very rare.
1142 —— Same, with half-cent. Fair lot. 3 p
1143 HALF-DIME; *very* fine; one of the best that I ever saw. Rare.
1144 DIME. Fine; very scarce.
1145 QUARTER-DOLLAR. Ordinary.
1146 HALF-DOLLAR, from the die of 1804. Fair for variety now scarce.
1148 —— Same; new die. Better than last.

United States Coins. 73

1806.

1149 Cent; fine for date, seldom better. Scarce.
1150 Half-cent. Fine.
1151 Quarter-dollars. Good. 2 p
1152 Half-dollar. Good.

1807.

1153 Cent; die of 1806, and new die. Fair. 2 p
1154 Half-cent. Fair.
1155 Dime. *Very* fine for date; scarce.
1156 Quarter-dollar. Fair.
1157 Half-dollar; head to r. Good.
1158 —— Same; new die; head to l. Good.

1808.

1159 Cent. A very good impression; sharp, but dark; scarce.
1160 —— Same; 12 stars; same description.
1161 Half-cent. Fair.
1162 Half-dollar. Fine.

1809.

1163 Cent. Very fair, even fine for date, now very scarce.
1164 Half-cent. Fine.
1165 Dime. In ordinary condition; scarce.
1166 Half-dollar. Fine.

1810.

1167 Cent; die of 1809. Sharp and fine; dark.
1168 Half-cent. Fine.
1169 Half-dollar. Very fine.

1811.

1170 Cent; die of 1810. Ordinary.
1171 —— Same; new die. Extremely fine impression, but has been cleaned.
1172 Half-cent. Fine for date; scarce.
1173 Dime. Ordinary, but scarce.
1174 Half-dollar. Very fine.

74   *American.*

1812.
1175 CENT. Fine; dark.
1176 HALF-DOLLAR. Very fine.

1813.
1177 CENT. Fine; dark.
1178 HALF-DOLLAR. Very fine.

1814.
1179 CENT. Fine; dark.
1180 DIME. Very fine for this date; rare in this condition.
1181 HALF-DOLLAR. Fine.

1815.
1182 QUARTER-DOLLAR. Uncommonly fine; very rare in this condition.
1183 —— Same. Fine.
1184 HALF-DOLLAR. Good for date.

1816.
1185 CENT. Broken die; red and uncirculated.
1186 —— Same; perfect die. Very fine; scarce.
1187 HALF-DOLLAR. Extremely fine; scarce.

1817.
1188 CENT; 13 stars. Uncirculated.
1189 —— Same; 15 stars. Nearly uncirculated; scarce.
1190 HALF-DOLLAR. Very fine.

1818.
1191 CENT. Uncirculated.
1192 QUARTER-DOLLAR. Uncirculated; scarce.
1193 HALF-DOLLAR (over 1817). Fine.
1194 —— Same; varieties. Very fine.   2 p

1819.
1195 CENT. Red and uncirculated.
1196 —— Same. Same condition; different.
1197 HALF-DOLLARS. Very fine.   2 p

United States Coins. 75

1820.

1198 CENT. Uncirculated; brilliant; rare.
1199 —— Same. Nearly uncirculated; different.
1200 DIMES. *Very* fine; varieties.
1201 QUARTER-DOLLAR. Equally fine.
1202 HALF-DOLLAR. Proof impression; slightly circulated; very desirable.
1203 —— Same. Fine.

1821.

1204 CENT. Only slight marks of circulation, and an *extremely* fine impression; rare.
1205 DIME. Very fine; scarce.
1206 QUARTER-DOLLAR. Very fine.
1207 HALF-DOLLAR. Very fine.

1822.

1208 CENT. Beautiful proof; extremely rare.
1209 —— Same. Extremely fine; slightly circulated; rare.
1210 —— Same. Equally fine; different die.
1211 DIME. Good for date; scarce.
1212 QUARTER-DOLLAR. Good for date.
1213 HALF-DOLLAR. Extremely fine.

1823.

1214 CENT. Much better than usually offered even in a good collection, always a difficult date to fill; scarce.
1215 —— Same. More circulated.
1216 —— Same. Re-struck; bright; scarce.
1217 DIME. *Very* fine; scarce.
1218 QUARTER-DOLLAR. Very fine; certainly the second best that I remember; rare to excess.
1219 HALF-DOLLAR. Very fine.

1824.

1220 DIME. Good for date.
1221 QUARTER-DOLLAR. Good for date; scarce.
1222 HALF-DOLLAR. Extremely fine.
1223 —— Same. Proof impression; a little circulated.
1224 —— Same. Very fine.

76 *American.*

1825.

1225 CENT. Very fine; barely circulated; rare.
1226 DIME. Proof impression; short scratch behind bust; very desirable; rare.
1227 —— Same. Very fine.
1228 QUARTER-DOLLAR. Very fine.
1229 HALF-DOLLAR. Very fine.

1826.

1230 CENT. Extremely fine; but little circulated; rare.
1231 HALF-CENT. Same.
1232 HALF-DOLLAR. Same.

1827.

1233 CENT. Uncirculated; fine olive color; very rare.
1234 —— Same. Very fine.
1235 DIME. Very fine; scarce.
1236 QUARTER-DOLLAR. Brilliant proof; with the exception of the 1823, the rarest of the quarters.
1237 HALF-DOLLAR. Fine *proof;* very rare.

1828.

1238 CENT. Only fair.
1239 HALF-CENT. Uncirculated; bright; scarce.
1240 —— Same. Fine.   2 p
1241 HALF-DIME. Very fine.
1242 DIME. Proof; a little circulated; rare.
1243 QUARTER-DOLLAR. Fine.
1244 HALF-DOLLAR. Extremely fine.

1829.

1245 CENT. Very fine; dark.
1246 HALF-CENT. Very fine.
1247 DIME. Proof; very rare.
1248 HALF-DOLLAR. Uncirculated; brilliant.

United States Coins.

1830.
- 1249 Cent. Ordinary.
- 1250 Half-dime. Fine.
- 1251 Dime. Very fine.
- 1252 Half-dollar. Fine.

1831.
- 1253 Cent. Fine.
- 1254 Half-dime. Uncirculated.
- 1255 Dime. Uncirculated.
- 1256 Quarter-dollar. Proof; slightly circulated; rare.
- 1257 —— Same. Very fine.
- 1258 Half-dollar. Uncirculated; brilliant.

1832.
- 1259 Cent. Uncirculated, but with slight scratches.
- 1260 Half-cent. Very fine.
- 1261 Half-dime. Uncirculated.
- 1262 Dime. Uncirculated.
- 1263 Quarter-dollar. Fine.
- 1264 Half-dollar. Very fine.

1833.
- 1265 Cent. Fine impression and color; slightly circulated.
- 1266 Half-cent. Uncirculated.
- 1267 Half-dime. Extremely fine.
- 1268 Dime. Very fine.
- 1269 Quarter-dollar. Very fine.
- 1270 Half-dollar. Same condition.

1834.
- 1271 Cent. Fine impression and color; nearly uncirculated.
- 1272 —— Same. Fine (a variety).
- 1273 Half-cent. Fine.
- 1274 Half-dime. Extremely fine.
- 1275 Dime. Equally fine.
- 1276 Quarter-dollar. Proof impression, circulated.
- 1277 Half-dollar. Large date; ex. fine.
- 1278 —— Same. Small date; equally fine.

1835.

1279 CENT. Fine; circulated.
1280 HALF-CENT. Uncirculated.
1281 —— Same; fine.
1282 HALF-DIMES. Very fine. 2 p
1283 DIMES. Very fine.
1284 QUARTER-DOLLARS. Very fine. 2 p
1285 HALF-DOLLAR. Very fine.

1836.

1286 CENT. Broken die; nearly uncirculated.
1287 HALF-CENT (pattern); brilliant proof. Very rare.
1288 HALF-DIME. Very fine.
1289 DIME. Very fine.
1290 QUARTER-DOLLAR. Very fine.
1291 HALF-DOLLAR. Very fine.
1292 DOLLAR (pattern); proof, slightly circulated. Rare.
1292* —— Same in gold (also a pattern); Liberty-cap; rev. 1 D; brilliant proof. Rare.

1837.

1283 CENT. Uncirculated; red.
1294 —— Same; different die. Nearly as fine.
1295 HALF-CENT worth of pure copper; Dr. Feuchtwanger's cent. Very fine. 2 p
1296 HALF-DIMES; two varieties. Very fine; scarce. 2 p
1297 DIMES; same. Ex. fine. 2 p
1298 QUARTER-DOLLAR; brilliant. Scarce.
1299 HALF-DOLLAR. Ex. fine.

1838.

1300 CENT; uncirculated; bright red.
1301 HALF-DIME. Very fine.
1302 DIMES; two varieties. One very fine. 2 p
1303 QUARTER-DOLLARS; two varieties. Very fine. 2 p
1304 HALF-DOLLAR. Fine.

United States Coins. 79

1839.

1305 CENT; head of '38; *uncirculated*. Rare.
1306 —— Same; booby head; ex. fine for variety. Rare.
1307 —— Same; head of '40; sharp; very fine. Rare.
1308 HALF-DIME. Very fine.
1309 DIMES. Extremely fine. 2 p
1310 QUARTER-DOLLAR. Very fine.
1311 HALF-DOLLAR; fine.
1312 DOLLAR (pattern); has been circulated and rubbed, but not to a great extent. Very desirable and extremely rare.

1840.

1313 CENT; ordinary.
1314 HALF-CENT (pattern); fine proof, beautiful steel color. Rare.
1315 HALF-DIME. Very fine.
1316 DIME; struck proof; slightly circulated.
1317 QUARTER-DOLLARS; very fine, one N. O. Mint. 2 p
1318 HALF-DOLLARS; one N. O. mint. Very fine. 2 p
1319 DOLLAR; fine proof; has received a few slight scratches, *very* slight; a beautiful dollar. Rare.

1841.

1320 CENT; strictly fine proof. Very rare.
1321 HALF-CENT (pattern); brilliant proof. Rare.
1322 —— Same; uncirculated. Scarce.
1323 HALF-DIME; fine.
1324 DIMES; two varieties; one N. O. and nearly proof. 2 p
1325 QUARTERS; same (one N. O. mint.) Very fine. 2 p
1326 DOLLAR; splendid impression; nearly proof. Rare.

1842.

1328 CENT; large date; splendid proof. Very rare.
1329 HALF-CENT (pattern); brilliant proof. Excessively rare.
1330 CENT; fine.
1331 HALF-DIME. Very fine.

1332 DIME. Extremely fine.
1333 QUARTER-DOLLARS (one N. O. mint). Very fine. 2 p
1334 HALF-DOLLAR. Very fine.
1335 DOLLAR. Very fine.

1843.

1336 CENTS; two varieties. Very fine. 2 p
1337 HALF-CENT (pattern); brilliant proof. Rare.
1338 HALF-DIME. Very fine.
1339 DIME; beautiful impression; nearly proof.
1340 QUARTER-DOLLAR. Extremely fine.
1341 HALF-DOLLAR. Very fine.
1342 DOLLAR. Fine.

1844.

1343 CENT; uncirculated, red color. Scarce.
1344 HALF-CENT (pattern); brilliant proof. Rare.
1345 HALF-DIME; fine for date. Scarce.
1346 DIME; good for date.
1347 QUARTER-DOLLAR. Fair.
1348 HALF-DOLLAR. Very fine.
1349 DOLLAR. Fine.

1845.

1350 CENT; fine, nearly uncirculated.
1351 HALF-CENT (pattern); brilliant proof. Rare.
1352 HALF-DIME; extremely fine. Scarce.
1353 DIME; equally fine.
1354 QUARTER-DOLLAR. Very fine.
1355 HALF-DOLLAR. Extremely fine.
1356 DOLLAR; equally fine. Very scarce.

1846.

1357 CENT, uncirculated; bright red.
1358 HALF-CENT (pattern); brilliant proof. Rare.
1359 HALF-DIME; fine for date. Very scarce.
1360 DIME; very fine. Scarce.
1361 QUARTER-DOLLAR. Equally fine.
1362 HALF-DOLLAR. Same.

United States Coins. 81

1363 Dollar; splendid proof, with a few very light touches, just discernible. Beautiful and rare.
1364 —— Same; fair impression.
1364*Set of silver coins of this year (5 pieces); nearly proof. Very rare.

1847.

1365 Cent, uncirculated; bright red.
1366 Half-cent (pattern); brilliant proof. *Very rare.*
1367 Half-dime. Extremely fine.
1368 Dime. Equally fine.
1369 Quarter-dollar. Same.
1370 Half-dollar. Ordinary.
1371 Dollar. Very fine.
1371*Set of the silver coins of this year, dollar, half do. quarter, dime, and half-dime; proof, with slight marks of circulation, still extremely fine and rare, and very desirable.

1848.

1372 Cent; splendid proof. Very scarce.
1373 Half-cent (pattern); brilliant proof. Rare.
1374 Dime. Very fine.
1375 Quarter-dollar. Very fine.
1376 Half-dollar (N. O. mint). Fine.
1377 Dollar; nearly proof; slightly circulated.
1377*Set, same as 1371*, with the addition of a cent, bright red. Very fine and rare.

1849.

1378 Cent; uncirculated.
1379 Half-cent; uncirculated.
1380 Half-dime. Extremely fine.
1381 Dime. Very fine.
1382 Quarter-dollar. Extremely fine.
1383 Half-dollar. Extremely fine.
1383*Dollar, nearly proof; very desirable.
1384 Set of silver of this date; nearly proof. 5 p

82   *American.*

1850.

- 1385 CENTS; uncirculated.   2 p
- 1386 —— Same (pattern); in centre a ring (not punched); struck in nickel; proof. Very rare.
- 1387 HALF-CENT. Fine.
- 1388 THREE cents; Liberty cap (pattern); fine proof. Rare.
- 1389 HALF-DIME. Fine.
- 1390 DIME. Very fine.
- 1391 QUARTER-DOLLAR. Very fine.
- 1392 HALF-DOLLAR. Very fine, little circulated.
- 1393 DOLLAR; proof impression; slightly circulated.

1851.

- 1394 CENT, uncirculated; bright red.
- 1395 —— Same (pattern) CENT within wreath; rev. same as silver coins of this date; copper, bright proof. Size 13
- 1396 HALF-CENTS; uncirculated.   2 p
- 1397 THREE cents; uncirculated, brilliant. Rare.
- 1398 HALF-DIME. Extremely fine.
- 1399 DIME. Fine.
- 1400 QUARTER-DOLLAR. Fine.
- 1401 HALF-DOLLAR. Fine.
- 1402 DOLLAR (gold). Fine, scarce.

1852.

- 1403 CENTS; uncirculated; (2 bright).   3 p
- 1404 HALF-CENT (pattern); brilliant proof. Rare.
- 1405 THREE cents; uncirculated.
- 1406 HALF-DIME; ordinary.
- 1407 DIME. Very fine.
- 1408 QUARTER-DOLLAR. Equally fine.

1853.

- 1409 CENTS; uncirculated; bright red.   2 p
- 1410 HALF-CENT. Fine.
- 1411 THREE cents. Very fine.
- 1412 HALF-DIMES; both varieties. Very fine.   2 p

United States Coins. 83

1413 DIME; same, with and without arrow-heads; uncirculated.
2 p
1414 QUARTER-DOLLAR; same. Very fine. 2 p
1415 HALF-DOLLAR; uncirculated. Scarce.
1416 DOLLAR; extremely fine; a beautiful impression, very little circulated. Rare.

1854.

1417 CENT; uncirculated. Bright red.
1418 —— Same; *brilliant* proof. Very rare.
1419 —— Same (pattern); head of Liberty without stars. Scarce.
1420 HALF-cent. Very fine.
1421 THREE cents. Uncirculated.
1422 HALF dime. Very fine.
1423 DIME. Extremely fine.
1424 QUARTER-dollar. Very fine.
1425 HALF-dollar; splendid impression, and nearly proof. Very scarce.
1426 DOLLAR; fine for this date. Very scarce.

1855.

1427 CENTS; date upright, and date oblique. Bright red. 2 p
1428 HALF-cent. Uncirculated.
1429 THREE cents. Uncirculated.
1430 HALF-dime. Very fine.
1431 DIME. Same.
1432 QUARTER dollar. Uncirculated.
1433 HALF-dollar. Very fine.

1856.

1434 CENTS, uncirculated; bright red. Large copper. 2 p
1435 —— Same; brilliant proof. Very rare.
1436 —— Same; nickel (pattern); fine proof. Very rare.
1437 HALF-cent. Uncirculated.
1438 THREE cents. Very fine.
1439 HALF-dime. Very fine.

84   *American.*

1440 DIMES, large and small date; very fine. Scarce.   2 p
1441 QUARTER-dollar. Very fine.
1442 HALF-dollar. Very fine.

1857.

1443 CENT; brilliant proof. Very rare.
1444 HALF-cent; brilliant proof. Rare.
1445 CENT and half-cent. Uncirculated.   2 p
1446 —— Same; nickel. Uncirculated.
1447 SET of the silver coins of this date; the dollar, a proof impression; the other five pieces very fine; there are a few light marks of circulation on the dollar. It is, however, very desirable.   6 p

1858.

1448 CENT. Uncirculated.
1449 —— Same; two varieties of the patterns of this date. Fine proof.   2 p
1450 THREE cents. Very fine.
1451 HALF-dime. Very fine.
1452 DIME. Equally fine.
1453 QUARTER; *brilliant* proof. Very rare.
1454 HALF-dollar. Very fine (N. O. mint.)
1455 PROOF set, seven pieces; brilliant, and a perfect set. Rare.

1859.

1456 CENT; fine proof. Scarce.
1457 THREE cents. Very fine.
1458 HALF-dime; brilliant proof. Scarce.
1459 DIME. Uncirculated.
1460 QUALTER-dollar. Proof.
1461 HALF-dollar. Brilliant proof.
1462 DOLLAR. Brilliant proof.
1463 PROOF set, seven pieces. Brilliant.

United States Coins. 85

1860.

1464 Cent. Fine proof.
1465 Three cents. Fine proof.
1466 Half-dime. Very fine.
1467 Dime. Same.
1468 Quarter-dollar. Uncirculated.
1469 Dollar. Brilliant proof.
1470 Proof set. Brilliant.   7 p

1861.

1471 Cent. Uncirculated.
1472 Three cents. Same.
1473 Half-dime. Very fine.
1474 Quarter-dollar. Fine.
1475 Dollar. Brilliant proof.
1476 Proof set. Brilliant.   7 p
1477 —— Same; including *gold* dollar. All brilliant.   8 p

1862.

1478 Cent. Uncirculated.   2 p
1479 Three cents. Proof.
1480 Half-dime. Uncirculated.
1481 Dime. Same.
1482 Quarter-dollar. Brilliant proof.
1483 Half-dollar. Same.
1484 Dollar. Same.
1485 Proof set. Brilliant.   7 p

1863.

1486 Cents. Fine proof.   2 p
1487 Two cents (pattern in bronze); GOD OUR TRUST; fine proof. Scarce.   2 p
1488 Same in nickel; thick planchet; brilliant proof. Rare.
1489 Same, with head of George Washington; splendid proof; nickel; thick planchet. Very rare.
1490 Same in bronze.

86 *American.*

1491 Three cents; pattern in bronze; head of Liberty within a circle of stars, 1863; rev. within a wreath, 3 CENTS; brilliant proof. Size 17

1492 Postal Currency; 10 CENTS; in aluminum. Very rare.

1493 Same it aluminum and silver; different proportions. (Pattern). 2 p

1494 Same, in bronze. Rare.
1495 Three cents. Fine proof.
1496 Half-dime. Uncirculated.
1497 Dime. Brilliant proof.
1498 Quarter-dollar. Same.
1499 Half-dollar. Very fine.
1500 Dollar. Brilliant proof.

1864.

1501 Cents; bronze and nickel. Fine proofs. 2 p
1502 Two cents; bronze, regular issue. Proof.
1503 Same; struck on thick nickel planchet. Rare.
1504 Half-dime. Fine proof.
1505 Dime. Same.
1506 Quarter-dollar. Same.
1507 Half-dollar. Same.
1508 Dollar. Same.
1509 Proof set. Fine proofs. 9 p

1865.

1510 Cent. Uncirculated.
1511 Two cents. Brilliant proof.
1512 Same. Uncirculated.
1513 Three cents. Same.
1514 Half-dime. Brilliant proof.
1515 Dime. Same.
1516 Quarter-dollar. Same.
1517 Half-dollar. Same.
1518 Dollar. Same.

1866.

CENT. Uncirculated.
SAME. Brilliant proof.
Two cents. Uncirculated.
SAME. Brilliant proof.
THREE cents; nickel. Fine proof.
FIVE cents (pattern); head of Washington, IN GOD
  WE TRUST; rev. within laurel wreath, 5; Nickel;
  fine proof. Rare.   Size 16
PROOF set of the nickel and copper coins of this year,
  viz.: 5, 3, 2, and 1 cent. Brilliant.
THREE cents (silver). Fine proof.
HALF-DIME (silver). Same.
DIME. Same.
QUARTER-DOLLAR. Uncirculated.
HALF-DOLLAR. Very fine.
DOLLAR. Brilliant proof.
PROOF set. Brilliant.
SAME, with gold dollar. Rare.

1867.

CENT. Uncirculated.
Two cents. Same.
SAME. Brilliant proof.
FIVE cents; nickel. Uncirculated.
SAME (pattern); Longacre's head of Liberty; rev. large
  V.; in aluminum; fine proof. Very rare.
THREE cents (silver). Proof.
HALF-DIME. Same.
DIME. Same.
QUARTER-DOLLAR. Same.
HALF-DOLLAR. Same.
DOLLAR. Same.

1868.

CENT. Uncirculated.
Two cents. Same.

1547 THREE cents. Brilliant proof.
1548 HALF-dime. Uncirculated.
1549 DIME. Very fine.
1550 QUARTER-dollar. Brilliant proof.
1551 HALF-dollar. Same.
1552 DOLLAR. Same.
1553 SET patterns, in nickel; five, three and one cent; obv. head of Liberty; reverses, large V., III. and I. within laurel wreath; proofs. Rare.
1554 DIME; struck in Aluminum. Very rare.
1555 GOLD dollar in same. Very rare.
1556 SMALL set proofs, nickel and copper. 4 p
1557 PROOF set; full. Brilliant. 10 p

1869.

1558 CENT. Uncirculated.
1559 Two cents. Same.
1560 FIVE cents; nickel. Brilliant proof.
1560* THREE cents (silver). Same.
1561 HALF-dime. Uncirculated.
1562 DIME. Brilliant proof.
1563 QUARTER-dollar. Same.
1564 HALF-dollar. Same.
1565 DOLLAR. Same.
1566 SET patterns, in nickel, five, three, and one cents (same as No. 1553). Fine proofs.
1567 SMALL set proofs, nickel and copper. 4 p
1568 PROOF set. Brilliant. 10 p

1870.

1569 CENT. Uncirculated.
1570 Two cents. Same.
1571 FIVE cents (nickel). Same.
1572 THREE cents (silver). Brilliant proof.
1573 HALF-dime. Same.
1574 DIME. Fine.
1575 QUARTER. Brilliant proof.

United States Coins. 89

1576 HALF-dollar. Same.
1577 DOLLAR. Same.
1578 SMALL set proofs, nickel and copper. 4 p
1579 PROOF set. Brilliant. 10 p

1871.

1580 CENT. Uncirculated.
1581 Two cents. Same.
1582 HALF-dime. Fine.
1583 DIME. Same.
1584 QUARTER-dollar. Brilliant proof.
1585 HALF-dollar. Same.
1586 DOLLAR. Same.
1587 PROOF set. Brilliant. 10 p

1872.

1588 CENT. Brilliant proof.
1589 Two cents. Same.
1590 THREE cents (nickel). Same.
1591 FIVE cents (nickel). Same.
1592 HALF-dime. Very fine.
1593 DIME. Fine.
1594 QUARTER-dollar. Brilliant proof.
1595 HALF-dollar. Same.
1596 PROOF set. Brilliant. 10 p

1873.

1597 CENT. Brilliant proof.
1598 —— Same. Uncirculated. 2 p
1599 THREE cents; nickel. Fine proof.
1600 FIVE cents; nickel. Same. 2 p
1601 THREE cents; silver. Same.
1602 HALF-dime. Fine.
1603 DIME. Same.
1604 —— Same; arrow heads to r. and l. of date. Very fine.
1605 QUARTER-dollar. Brilliant proof.
1606 —— Same; arrows, etc. Very fine.

1607 HALF-dollar. Fine proof.
1608 —— Same, with arrows, etc. Very fine.
1609 DOLLAR ; old type. Fine and scarce.
1610 —— Same ; new type. Brilliant proof.
1611 SMALL set proofs, nickel and copper. 4 p
1612 PROOF set ; old type ; brilliant. Very rare. 10 p

[As few collectors of coins will ever have an opportunity to see a set of the patterns out of which the "Trade Dollar" was selected (or rather out of which it *grew*, because it is different from any one of the six before me), I will mention here their characteristics and then catalogue them separately, reserving the right to sell them in this way or as a set. They all have on the principal side a representation of the Goddess of Liberty in some form, and on the reverse the usual motto and legend, with the addition of "420 grains, 900 fine." with the title—TRADE DOLLAR.]

1613 DOLLAR ; head crowned with a *vine ;* rev. eagle on a mountain-top supporting shield and motto upright.
1614 Same ; head of Liberty ; rev. inscription within a wreath of laurel.
1615 Same ; Liberty seated on a globe ; rev. similar to, though not the same as 1613.
1616 Same ; obverse resembling last ; rev. smaller eagle on a shield.
1617 Same ; Liberty seated on bales of merchandise, in her right hand sprig of olive ; rev. small eagle on a mountain-top.
1618 Same ; Liberty seated on a globe ; on her head a tiara of feathers ; rev. eagle displayed, in his talons darts and olive branch.

[All brilliant proofs and exceedingly rare.]

1874.

1619 CENT. Brilliant proof. 2 p
1620 THREE cents ; nickel. Same.
1621 FIVE cents ; nickel. Same.
1622 QUARTER-dollar. Same.
1623 DOLLAR. Brilliant proof.
1624 PROOF set ; full. Brilliant. 7 p

Medals. 91

1875.

1625 CENT. Brilliant proof 2 p
1626 THREE cents. Same.
1627 FIVE cents. Same.
1628 DIME. Same.
1629 QUARTER-dollar. Same.
1630 HALF-dollar. Same.
1631 DOLLAR. Same.
1632 PROOF set. Brilliant. 7 p

CONFEDERACY.

1633 CENT; head in Phrygian cap, CONFEDERATE STATES OF AMERICA, 1861; rev. within a wreath of rice, cotton and tobacco, 1 CENT; copper; fine proof. Very rare. Size 12

1634 SERIES of cents without the rare dates. Many of them fine. 60 p
1635 —— Same. Nearly equal to last. 60 p
1636 —— Same. Half-cents. 31 p

MEDALS.

[Either relating to America or American.]

1637 CAROLINA medal, 1736 (for description see No. 538); splended uncirculated impression. Silver.
1638 LIBERTAS Americana, July, 1776; rev. Pallas defending America; fine proof impression; strictly uncirculated. Bronze. Size 30
1639 —— Same; rev. *Communiconsensu*, 1783; tin with copper plug; proof. Rare. Size 28
1640 GERMAN-American medal; by *Calker;* three figures standing; Mercury descending; silver-gilt proof. Rare. Size 28
1641 JOHN PAUL JONES, 1779; *Dupre;* bronze. Not in perfect order. Size 36
1641* WILLIAM BAINBRIDGE, 1812; by *Furst*. Bronze proof. Size 36
1642 W— BURROWS, 1813; by *Furst*. Bronze proof. Size 36

92   *American.*

1643 DECATUR and Lawrence; by *Furst*, 1813; military busts of both; nearly proof; tin. Rare.   Size 22
1644 LAFAYETTE, "The defender of American and French liberty, 1777, 1824." Bronze proof, by *Caumois*.
                                                                Size 29
1645 —— Young bust; rev. French inscription, "He commanded the National Guard in 1789-90-91;" by *Dumarest;* fine proof, bronze. Rare.   Size 22

MEDALS AND MEDALETS, WITH BUSTS.

[All very fine.]

GEORGE WASHINGTON.

1646 HALF-dollar, 1792; Idler's Copy, in tin; proof.
1647 SUCCESS to the United States; brass. Unusually fine.
                                                                Size 16
1648 BUST of Washington, with Abraham's card; uncirculated. Rare.
1649 —— Rev. National monument, 1848; tin.   Size 24
1650 —— Rev. tomb; *Merriam;* tin.   Size 20
1651 —— Rev. "Mouran;" brass.   Size 20
1652 —— Rev. Patriæ Pater; *Key;* tin.   Size 18
1653 —— Rev. head of Jackson; silver.   Size 12
1654 COPPERHEADS and spiel marks.   15 p

BENJAMIN FRANKLIN (*reverses*).

1655 TIME is Money. By *Merriam;* copper proof. Size 20
1656 —— Same, in tin.
1657 COPPERHEAD (bust of Franklin).

MAJ.-GEN. WAYNE.

1658 MILITARY bust, cocked hat; rev. battle-field. *Robinson's* series; fine proof, copper.   Size 22

ROBERT FULTON.

1659 BUST bare; rev. "Steam Navigation, etc." Robinson's series.

DAVID HOSACK.

1660 BUST; rev. "Arts and Science." By *Furst;* fine proof, bronze.   Size 21

Medals and Medalets, with Busts. 93

Gen. Jackson.

1661 Medal voted by Congress; rev. "Peace and Friendship;" bronze, proof. Size 32
1662 Medalets in brass; head right, left, and front; unusually fine. 3 p

M. Van Buren.

1663 Bust three-quarter face; rev. National Union League, 1863; copper, bright. Size 16
1664 —— Same, in brass.

Henry Clay.

1665 Small bust. By *Thomas;* THE FARMER OF ASHLAND; rev. ins., May 1, 1844; fine proof, tin. Size 24
1666 —— Same; rev. Bunker Hill, etc.; same.
1667 Medals in tin. By Merriam and another. 2 p
1668 —— Rev. scales; rev. Mill boy of the Slashes and Shell. 3 p
1669 Others in brass; extremely fine lot, no duplicates. 6 p

Daniel Webster.

1670 Bust. By *Merriam;* rev. "I Still Live;" tin proof. Size 19
1671 —— Same; Hill's card; tin proof.

Louis Kossuth.

1672 Medalets in brass; fine condition, 3 varieties.

Edwin Forrest.

1673 Bust. By *Merriam;* rev. "Rose by his own efforts;" fine proof, copper. Size 19
1674 —— Same, in tin.

Wm. Henry Harrison.

1675 Military bust; rev. "Battle of the Thames, 1813;" strictly uncirculated impression, copper. Rare.
1676 Bare head. By *Mitchell;* rev. Monument, Bunker Hill Jubilee, Sept. 10, 1840; original impression, tin, nearly proof. Rare.

1677 Bust in civilian dress, "To the Hero of Tippecanoe;" rev. Bunker Hill Monument; copper proof. Size 24
1678 Same; rev. residence; proof of copper. Size 22
1679 Same, in tin.
1680 Military bust; rev. log cabin; on thick planchet; copper proof. Size 20
1681 —— Same, in tin.
1682 Medalets in brass; extra fine lot. 5 p

Winfield Scott.

1683 Bust. By Leonard; rev. "A Gallant and Skillful Hero;" tin. Size 26
1684 Bust; "First in War, First in Peace;" brass. Size 18
1685 —— Rev. Vera Cruz, Cerro-Gordo, etc.; tin. Size 18
1686 —— Rev. Scott wounded, etc., and two others. 3 p

Zachery Taylor.

1686*Bust; rev. "I Ask no Favors," etc.; tin. Size 26

John C. Fremont.

1687 Bust; rev. "Honor to whom Honor is Due;" tin. Size 24
1688 —— Same, ¾ face; rev. "Fremont & Cochrane;" tin. Size 22
1689 Bust; rev. "Free Soil and Free Speech;" tin. Size 20
1690 Tokens in brass. 2 p

Franklin Pierce.

1691 Bust. By Leonard; rev. "United we Stand;" tin. Size 26
1692 Medalet in brass. Very fine.

Polk & Dallas.

1693 Political medal, with their busts vis-a-vis; tin. Size 28

James Buchanan.

1694 Bust; rev. "The Crisis Demands, etc." By S. & H., tin. Size 22
1695 Medalet in brass.

Stephen A. Douglas.

1696 Bust. By *Childs*, of Chicago; rev. inscription, tin.
Size 24
1697 —— By *True*; rev. eagle; lead. Size 24
1698 Medalets in copper and brass; fine and rare, 4 varieties.

John Bell.

1699 Political tokens, with his bust; 4 varieties.

Abraham Lincoln.

1700 Bust. By *Merriam*; rev. "No More Slave Territory;" copper proof. Size 20
1701 —— Same, in tin.
1702 —— Same, smaller, copper. Size 17
1703 Bust. By *Ellis*; rev. rail-splitting; copper. Size 18
1704 —— Same, in brass and tin. 2 p
1705 Bust. By R. L.(ovett); rev. "Protection," etc.; copper and brass. Size 18. 2 p
1706 Busts of Lincoln & Johnson in two medallions; rev. Republican Candidates; tin. Size 28
1707 Bust; below 25; In God we Trust; rev. eagle and inscription, 1864; tin. Rare. Size 16
1708 Copperheads, with his bust alone, and with Johnson; some very *rare*; copper and brass. 7 p

George B. McClellan.

1709 Bust, by *Key*; rev. inscription within a wreath; at the bottom, bust of Washington; on thick planchet; tin.
Size 32
1710 Bust, by R. L(ovett); rev. "I am sworn to defend, etc.;" with similar by *Key*; 2 sizes; tin; from size 18 to 22. 3 p
1711 Bust; rev. monitor; thick planchet; copper. Fine.
Size 18
1712 Bust, by *Merriam*, 1863; rev. eagle, etc. Fine. " 20
1713 Medalets and copperheads. Some very rare. 11 p

Horatio Seymour, and Seymour and Blair.

1714 Campaign Medalets. 2 varieties.

U. S. GRANT.

1715 BUST, by *Bovy*, Geneva, Switzerland; rev. PATIENT OF TOIL, SERENE AMID ALARMS, INFLEXIBLE IN FAITH, INVICIBLE IN ARMS; splendid proof. Rare. Size 36
1716 BUST, by *Key*; rev. inscription within wreath; tin. Size 36
1717 BUST within circles and wreath of laurel; rev. shield, flags, and eagle; in copper and tin. Size 30. 2 p
1718 BUSTS of Grant and Colfax, by *Bolen*; rev. "Let us have peace;" fine. Bronze. Size 19
1719 MEDALETS, by *Ellis, Bolen, and Key*; brass and tin. 4 p
1720 SAME; in gutta-percha and medals of various kinds and sizes. Rare lot. 6 p

STONEWALL JACKSON.

1721 BUST, by *Cacque*; rev. inscription; tin. Size 34

W. T. SHERMAN.

1722 BUST; three-quarter face; rev. round disc radiated; copper. Size 19

PHILIP KEARNEY.

1723 PROFILE bust, by *Merriam*; rev. eagle, etc.; copper. Rare. Size 20

EDWARD, PRINCE OF WALES.

1724 MEDAL; in commemoration of his visit to America; bust; rev. the Welsh plumes; in copper, brass, and tin; by *Merriam*. Size 20. 3 p

COL. JAMES FISK.

1725 BUST; rev. Locomotive; "Relief for Chicago;" brass. By *A. Willemin*. Very rare. Size 15

1726 DANIEL O'CONNELL, 1864; to commemorate the laying the first stone, etc.; brass. Size 10
1727 FRANCIS ASBURY; "Centenary of Methodism."
1728 J. A. BOLEN; die sinker. Very fine. Size 16
1729 STEPHEN GIRARD; full-length figure; rev. Lovett's card.

Commemoration Medals and Tokens.

Commemoration Medals and Tokens. (*All fine.*)

1730 Crystal Palace, N. Y., 1853 ; tin.   Size 34
1731 Emancipation Jubilee, 1834 ; tin.   " 30
1732 Rhode Island Industrial Exhibition ; rev. " Copy ;" tin.   Size 34
1733 Loyal National League ; white copper.   Size 26
1734 Boston City School Medal ; rev. "Helen A. Moore," 1866; silver.   Size 22
1735 Pennsylvania Volunteers ; Arms of the State, etc. ; tin.   Size 24
1736 New Masonic Temple, Boston ; dedicated June 24, A. L. 5867 ; C. C. Dame, G. M. ; tin.   Size 19
1737 Nassau Water Works ; Neptune seated ; tin.   " 20
1738 U. S. Arsenal ; *J. A. Bolen* ; tin.   " 18
1739 Great Eastern ; *Merriam* ; copper and tin. Size 18.   2 p
1740 Sabbath-School medal ; silver plated.   Size 22
1741 Lexington Centennial ; April 19, 1875 ; brass.   " 20
1742 —— Same ; in tin.
1743 Bunker Hill Centennial, June 17, 1775 ; tin.   Size 18
1744 Air Ship, City of New York ; rev. dimensions ; copper.   Size 22
1745 Sage's Historical tokens and odds and ends ; copper. 2 p
1746 North Point, and Fort McHenry, and Bolen's base ball club ; copper. Size 20.   2 p
1747 Atlantic Cable copper and tin. Size 18.   2 p
1748 Constitution and Guerriere ; Lovett's series ; plated and bronze.   2 p
1749 Fireman's Medal, 1860 ; copper and brass.   2 p
1750 Mobile Jockey Club, National Union League, and Hartford Wide-Awakes ; copper.   3 p
1751 Anti-tobacco ; Keep your Temper ; The wealth of the South ; Mass for Justice, etc.   6 p
1752 City Hall Spiel Marke ; Industry produces wealth, and other tokens.   6 p
1753 Ships Colonies and Commerce ; *Wright and Bales* ; and Yankee Robinson ; Masonic token. Both rare.   2 p
1754 " Good for a scent ; " dog's head ; various reverses and metals ; by *Merriam*.   5 p

1755 FIVE cent nickel tokens; Randall & Co.; Caracas, Eickstein & Co. 3 p
1756 BRIGHTON House; 5 cents, token; copper. Rare.

STORE CARDS, (*All fine.*)

1757 MOTT's Card, 1789; Ships Colonies & Commerce M. & B. 2 p
1758 SAME; with John J. Adams, Brushes. 2 p
1759 CROSSMAN's and Maycock's. 2 p
1760 SAME; with Clark & Anthony. 2 p
1761 CARRINGTON & Co. (Havana Express); A. S. Robinson; copper and brass. 3 p
1762 MOBILE Jockey Club, and Wm. W. Long. 2 p
1763 MULLIGAN (Watches); Richards (Att'y, Jewelry). 3 p
1764 CHUBBUCK (Utica); Faneuil Hall (Clothing). 2 p
1765 RICHARDSON, (3 umbrellas); Nath'l March, Portsmouth, N. H.; (with W. Simes on reverse). Rare. 2 p
1766 RUGGLES (gold beater); Willard (combs). 2 p
1767 PECK & BURNHAM; Henry Anderson. 2 p
1768 WALSH (Lansingburgh); varieties. 2 p
1769 ROBINSON & Co. (Buttons); and others. 6 p
1770 JENNINGS, Wheeler & Co.; varieties; brass. 5 p
1771 WOODGATE & Co.; represented by J. N. T. Bevick; copper; brilliant proof. Very rare.
1772 BURBANK & Shaw (Chicago). Very fine and rare.
1773 DOREMUS, Suydam & Nixon; by Bale & Smith. Extra fine and rare variety.
1774 J. A. BOLEN; Dickson, White & Co. (watches). 2 p.
1775 PROF. JOHNSON (small size, rare); Stephen Richardson, and others; all with heads. Rare lot. 5 p
1776 SAMUEL HART & Co.; Smith (clocks). Forbes & Barlow, and others. 10 p
1777 SUTT (distiller); Folger & Son (clothiers.) 2 p
1778 PEARSON & Dana (Chicago); Sise & Co., and others. 4 p
1779 A. WISE (dry goods); Christopher Karl, 42 Ave. A. (by Sigel). Rare. 2 p.
1780 SHARPLESS; W. Lyon & Co. (clothing.) 2 p
1781 M. B. ALLEBACH, jeweller, Phila. Nickel proof.
1782 JOHN FRANK (milk). Pint and one-half pint. 2 p

British Empire.

1783 ROXBURY coaches; new line, "J. Mitchell, People's Line." "Good for a ride in the 6th and 8th street omnibus line." 3 p
1784 FOSTER & MITCHEL (Grand Rapids); Stanwood & Co., Boston; Comers' Commercial College, Boston. Sic. Semper Tyrranis (button), etc. 10 p

1785 COPPERHEADS; two cent size. Bright. 12 p
1786 —— Cent size; no duplicate. Bright. 124 p
1787 SHINPLASTERS. Nearly all bright. 16 p
1788 —— Jackson; in brass. Very fine and rare.
1789 Box of copper coins. Unclassified. 200 p

BRITISH EMPIRE.
ENGLISH SILVER COINS.

1790 EDWARD III.; penny. Fine.
1791 MARY (Tudor) Groat; fine, but bent. Rare.
1792 ELIZABETH; shilling. *Extremely* fine.
1793 CHARLES I. Shilling, very fine and rare type, but notched.
1794 CHARLES II.; coronation medal, by *Simon*. Rare, but abused and circulated. Size 20
1795 CHARLES II.; crown. Very good.
1796 WILLIAM and MARY; half-crown. Fine.
1797 WILLIAM; sixpence. Very good.
1798 ANNA; half crown; very fine. Scarce.
1799 —— Shilling; roses and plumes. Very good.
1800 —— Duplicate. Ordinary.
1801 GEORGE II., shilling. Extremely fine.
1802 —— Sixpence. Fine.
1803 GEORGE III., dollar; Bank of England, 1804; extremely fine; nearly proof. Rare.
1804 — Same; Bank of Ireland: same date; fine. Rare.
1805 —— Two-third crown Brunswick; brilliant. Rare.
1806 —— Shilling, without dot in legend; fine; from the dies of 1787. *Very rare.*

1807 GEORGE III., Shilling, sixpence, threepence, twopence, and penny. Fine. 5 p
1808 —— Crown or medal, by *Droz*; struck 19th May, 1795; SOHO; beautiful proof. Rare.
1809 VICTORIA; florin. Fine.

ENGLISH COPPER COINS.
[A few brass tokens.]

1810 CHARLES S. Farthings. 2 p
1811 CHARLES II., bawbees. Scotch. 2 p
1812 —— FARTHING, CAROLVS A CARALO, 1672; nearly uncirculated. Rare.
1813 —— Duplicate. Equally fine.
1814 JAMES II.; gun money; crown of 1690. Fine.
1815 —— Medalet in brass; the King and Queen's head. Fine. Size 18
1816 WILLIAM III.; half-penny and farthing of Charles II. 2 p
1817 GEORGE I.; half-pennies (one Wood's.) 2 p
1818 GEORGE II.; farthing and token. Fine. 2 p
1819 —— Half-pennies. Very fine. 2 p
1820 GEORGE III.; two-penny, 1797; very fine. Scarce.
1821 —— Penny. Equally fine. Scarce.
1822 HALF-penny; uncirculated. Bright. 2 p
1823 —— Same, 1775 and 1807; uncirculated. Bright. 2 p
1824 —— Same, and farthings. 4 p
1825 —— Same, with bank and other tokens and pattern coins. Fine lot. 20 p
1826 GEORGE IV. and William IV. Farthings, etc. 6 p
1827 VICTORIA; coins and model crowns. Uncirculated and bright. 3 p
1828 —— Model coins and tokens. Fine. 13 p
1829 MISCELLANEOUS tokens; WE CONQUER TO SET FREE; Napoleon wending his way to Elba on an ass; Jubilee token 1688-1788, Canning; opening of the new London bridge 1831, etc. Fine and rare lot. 8 p

English Colonies.
Copper.

1830 SERRA Leone Company; cent, 1791; *fine* proof. Rare.
1831 LIBERIA and other anti-slavery tokens. Extra fine. 4 p
1832 —— "Am I not a man and a brother?" Bright, rare.
1833 EAST India and China. Beautiful lot. 10 p
1834 CEYLON Government; St. Helena, Bermuda, Demarara, and Jamaica. 6 p
1835 NOVA Scotia, Prince Edward's Island, and Canada CENTS and half-cents. Extra fine. 5 p
1836 NEW Foundland, Montreal, North America, New Brunswick, etc., penny and half-penny, tokens, and sous. Fine lot. 12 p
1837 SIMILAR lot. 12 p
1838 SIMILAR. More mixed. 16 p
1839 REPETITION of last. 15 p
1840 SHIPS, colonies, and commerce; Wellington token, O'Connell, speed the plough, Nova Scotia (J. Brown's card, Montreal sous, etc. Very fine. 12 p
1841 HENDON half-penny, with head of David Garrick; Menlough Castle sixpence (copper), and Isle of Man. 9 p

Trade Tokens.

1842 DRUID's head; penny and half-penny. Fine. 4 p
1843 HALF-pennies. Bright and uncirculated. 10 p
1844 RARE and artistic tokens, half-penny size; among them, "Pidcock's," with elephant, "lion, and dog," Lady Godiva, cow with two heads, St. Anthony of Padua, etc., etc. Very fine; uncirculated. 10 p
1845 HALF-PENNY, with religious texts, etc. 10 p
1846 —— Same, with busts; all fine. 10 p
1847 MISCELLANEOUS half-penny tokens. 21 p
1848 FARTHING tokens and medalets; beautiful, among them Wellington, "born and died." 6 p

British Empire.

English Medals.

1849 VERNON Medal, and two of the same character relating to the King of Prussia. 4 p

1850 GREAT Britain and Ireland united, 1800; beautiful bronze medal by *Hancock;* lion reposing on an anchor between the rose, shamrock, and thistle.
Size 24

1851 EARL SPENCER, bust; rev. Fame, 1799; bronze. Size 24

1852 BARON ROKEBY, Lord Primate of Ireland; fine bust. By *Mossop*; rev. church and text, 1788; bronze.
Size 33

1853 CHARLES I.; bust, by R.; rev. VIRTVT EX ME-FURTVNAM, etc.; bronze. Fine and rare.
Size 32

1854 FRENCH chapel; fine view of the edifice; rev. long ins.; bronze proof. Size 40

1855 SLAVE Trade abolished; we are all brethren; copper.
Size 24

1856 GEORGE III. on his recovery, etc.; tin. Size 23

1857 VICTORIA, to commemorate her visit with the Prince Consort to Liverpool, Oct., 1851; splendid medal; tin. Size 48

1858 —— By Bovy; Universal Exhibition, London, 1852; tin. Size 32

1859 PRINCE OF WALES and Princess Alexandria. *Ottley;* marriage at St. George Chapel, Dec. 1, 1863; splendid tin. Size 32

1860 MANCHESTER Exhibition of Art Treasures, 1857, and Kensington Exhibition, 1862, with Crystal Palace, 1851; beautiful medals in tin. 5 p

1861 GEORGE IV., Garibaldi, Tom Thumb, etc., etc.; same.
7 p

1862 VINCENT LUNARD, first ærial traveler in England, 1784; bust; rev. balloon; copper. Size 22

1863 GUINEA and other money weights. Fine. 4 p

FRANCE.

Silver Coins.

1864 Louis XV.; crown, 1757. Very fine.
1865 —— Small coin for Isles Du Vent. Fine.
1866 Louis XVI.; crown, 1786; extremely fine. Scarce.
1867 —— Half-crown; equally fine. Scarce.
1868 —— Quarter-crown; same. Scarce.
1869 —— Sixteenth-crown; same. Scarce.
1870 Louis XVIII.; five francs, 1822. Very fine.
1871 Charles X.; same. Very fine.
1872 Henry V.; one franc, 1831; not legitimate. Fine and extremely rare.
1873 Louis Philippe; five francs, 1831. Very fine.
1874 —— Same, 1834. Very fine.
1875 Republic; half-franc, 1850. Very fine.
1876 Napoleon III.; five francs, 1856. Ex. fine, scarce.
1877 —— One franc. Ex. fine.
1878 —— 50 centimes, and 20 do., 3 varieties.   3 p
1879 Republic; five francs, 1873. By *Dupre*. Very fine.

Copper Coins.

1880 Louis XIV. and XVI.; liard and two sous.   2 p
1881 Louis XVI., 1791–'92; old and new arms.   3 p
1882 Republic, 1793; siege of Mayence, etc.   4 p
1883 Monneroys; two and five sols. Very fine.   2 p
1884 Napoleon and Anvers; one decime and five centimes, 1815. Fine, very rare.   3 p
1885 Charles X., 1828; ten and five centimes. Extra fine.   4 p
1886 Louis Philippe, 1841; ten centimes.
1887 Republic and Napoleon III.; uncirculated.   6 p

Medals.

1888 War medal Napoleon III.; Expedition to Mexico; loop. Very fine and rare; silver.
1889 Series, Kings of France, by P.; first, second, and third race; obv. busts; rev. inscriptions. All fine. Size 20.   18 p

French Medals.

1890 LOUIS XIV. and his mother, Anna of Austria; their busts on opposite sides, with stem for ribbon; a superb bronze medal by *Warin*, 1643. Original and very rare. Size 36

1891 LOUIS XIV., on the capture of GRAVELINGA, 1644; bronze, by *Mauger*. Size 26

1892 NAPOLEON I. as First Consul; Peace of Luneville; fine medal by *Andrieu*; bronze. Size 25

1893 —— Souvenirs, with his full-length figure or bust in brass and copper. Fine. 3 p

1894 TOKENS of the old Republic; ovals, gilt. 2 p

1895 —— of the Revolution of 1830, by *Veyrat*; also gilt. 2 p

1896 LOUIS PHILIPPE, by *Montagne*; beautiful proof medalets. 2 p

1897 TOKENS of the Revolution of 1848; one with bust of Lamartine. Extra fine. 2 p

1898 NAPOLEON III., on his election by "acclamation" in 1851; on the birth of the young Prince; on the victory of Solferino, etc. 4 p

1899 —— Others on his election, etc.; splendid proofs in copper and brass. 2 p

1900 —— To commemorate his visit to England in 1855; in white metal. Size 34

1901 —— Busts of the Emperor and Empress; on the rev. head of the young Prince, 14th Jan., 1856; medalet in silver. Size 12

1902 LA FONTAINE; by *Gatteaux*; series metallic.

1903 POUSSIN; by *Dubois*; "

1904 HAYDN; by *Gatteaux*; "

1905 HENRY V., Duke of Orleans. 2 p

1906 ARMAND BARRE, Dupin, Genoude. Extra fine medals. Size 20. 3 p

1907 JETONS and medalets. 6 p

1908 MEDAL on the birth of a child, 29th Sept., 1820; by *Gayrard*; rev. angel trampling on a dragon; bronze. Size 24

Portugal—Brazil.

SPAIN—MEXICO.

Silver Coins.

1909 Charles III.; quarter-dollar, 1788.
1910 —— Dollar, 1792 (Mexican mint). Good.
1911 Charles IV.; same of 1806. *Very* fine.
1912 Ferdinand VII.; same, 1809; brilliant. Rare.
1913 Augustus I., Mexico (Iturbide); dollar; uncommonly fine impression. Rare.
1914 Mexican Republic, 1834; dollar. Very fine.
1915 Maximillian, Emperor, 1866; same. Very fine.
1916 —— Half-dollar. Extra fine.
1917 —— Ten and five cents. Rare. 2 p
1918 Republic, now existing; quarter-dollar and small silver coins. 4 p

1919 Copper coins of Ferdinand VII., etc. Fine lot. 7 p

PORTUGAL—BRAZIL.

Gold, Silver, and Copper Coins.

1920 John V.; ⅛ doubloon, 1744. Gold.
1921 John (?), 1813; dollar (960 R.) Very fine.
1922 Petrus V., 1859; 100 reis (10 cts.); uncirculated. Rare.
1923 Louis I., 1862; 200 reis; uncirculated. Rare.
1924 Copper "dump" of Joannes, 1812 (40 reis); one of the same denomination of Michael I., 1831. 2 p
1925 —— Handsome coins of old and recent dates; broad and fine. 10 p
1926 —— Same; fine lot. 5 p
1927 —— Selected to illustrate the monetary system of the Portuguese; it is to be hoped, that as the subject is important as well as interesting, it will receive proportionate attention from American financiers; LXXX R, 1822, XX, do., 1855; equally broad and thick (size 22); X.R, 1792; XL do., 1816, and 20

do., 1855; all of equal breadth and thickness (size 22); 5 R., 1843, and 2 do. of 1855; the last (2 reis) about four times the intrinsic value of the former (5 reis). This interesting group of seven pieces will be sold as one lot.

1928 PETER II., Brazil; set 1000-500; and 200 Reis, (intrinsic value about $1.00); the set.

CENTRAL AND SOUTH AMERICAN REPUBLICS, AND WEST INDIES.

1929 DOLLAR of the Rep. of C. America; 1831; five mountain peaks at sunrise; rev. tree. Very fine.

1930 —— Same of Bolivia; bust of Simon Bolivar; rev. two llamas under a tree; 1841. Very good.

1931 HALF-DOLLAR; same; base.

1932 SIXTEENTH-DOLLAR; same; fine. Very rare.

1933 Two Reals; Caracas; 1819. 2 p

1934 CAPE Tokens and Coins; the former beautiful; including set of Venezuela. 8 p

1935 DOLLAR of Peru; 1842. Fine.

1936 —— Same (1 Sol) of 1866. Extra fine.

1937 QUARTER; same issue. Rare.

1938 ONE Real; Chili; 1844. Fine.

1939 COPPERS of Chili. 2 p

1940 —— Same of Paraguay; one-twelfth (Real); lion beside a liberty-pole. Scarce.

1941 —— Same of Uruguay; 40, 20, and 5 centesmo, and one of 4. Extra fine. 4 p

1942 —— Same of Buenos Ayres; 1850. 5 p

1943 —— Same of Argentine Confederation.

1944 BASE Coins of Hayti; 50, 25, and 12 cents. 5 p

1945 COPPERS of same. Very fine and rare. 8 p

1946 ANTIGUA Farthing; (palm tree). Very rare.

1947 HAWAIIAN Rep.; Hapa-Haneri; 1847; uncir. Rare.

THE ORIENT, TURKEY, AND GREECE.

1948 COCHIN CHINA? broad, yellow coin; thick rim and square perforation. Size 28

Russia. 107

1949 TEMPO (Japan); similar but oblong.
1950 CASH (China). 7 p
1951 ITSBU; gold mixture and silver. 2 p
1952 JAPAN; quarter yen; obv., sun within an ornamental border of crysanthemum and other flowers and sprigs; rev. dragon and inscription; fine silver coin; value 25 cents. Rare.
1953 HONG KONG; Ten Cents; and Copper of Victoria. 2 p
1954 INDIA; quarter-rupee of same; and quarter and one-tenth guilder of Holland. Very fine. 3 p
1955 —— Beautiful uncirculated Dutch copper coins; 1857. 2 p
1956 —— Old Dutch Coppers. Fine. 3 p
1957 —— Copper, with Oriental inscription only. 5 p
1958 —— Thick copper of the Moguls. Rare.
1959 MOROCCO; double triangle; 2 sizes. 1 rare.
1960 TURKEY; fine silver; dime size.
1961 —— Large silver coin, supposed to be base. Fine.
1962 —— Uncirculated copper coins. Rare lot. 8 p
1963 TRIPOLI; copper coins. 2 p
1964 GREECE; copper; great variety; 10 Lepta, 5 Lepta, 2 Lepta, and 1 Lepta. 8 p
1965 —— Uncirculated 10 Para; 1866.

RUSSIA.

1966 PETER (The Great), 1725; copper of his last year. Rare. Size 19
1967 KATHARINE II., 1756; remarkable copper coin. Thick and fine. Size 20
1968 ELIZABETH PETROVNA, 1777; struck for Siberia; nearly uncirculated. Very rare. Size 22
1969 FIVE COPECS; large coppers; 1784 and 1794. Very fine. 2 p
1970 SILVER Medal; 1782; bust of Katharine II.; rev., statue of Peter the Great. Size 16
1971 Two Copecs; Alex. I., 1797 to 1800. 3 p
1972 FIVE Copecs; new and improved coinage. Very fine.

Sweden—Italy.

1973 ROUBLE of same (Alex. I.); 1834; struck by Nicholas; obv. bust; rev. monument; very fine. Rare.
1974 Two, One, and Half Copec; Alex. I. Ex. fine. 6 p
1975 OTHERS. 6 p
1976 ALEX. II.; Roumania; uncirculated. 2 p
1977 ROUBLE; fine silver; nearly uncir.; 1836. Scarce.
1977* HALF and Quarter Roubles. 2 p
1978 TWENTY, Ten, Five Copec, and Medalet. 4 p

SWEDEN.

1979 CHARLES XI.; two Marks (half-thaler); 1687. Very fine.
1980 CHARLES XIV.; dollar of 1824; bare bust; rev. arms crowned; 1 S. P.s; nine and one-fourth St. 1 Mk. F. S.; uncircuated. Rare.
1981 CHARLES XV.; half of last; same description; equally fine. Rare.
1982 OSCAR; dollar, 1856; bare bust; rev. arms on shield, supported by two lions; nearly equal to last.
1983 COPPER coins in great variety; without duplicates. All very fine. 12 p

1984 BELGIUM copper coins, 5 cent, 2 cent, 1 cent; uncirculated. 3 p
1985 —— Same; with Wurtemberg and other German coins; bright and uncirculated. 12 p
1986 GERMAN Coins, generally fine; copper. 22 p
1987 HOLLAND; pure copper, cut from a bar; 2 S(tivers) and 1 S(tiver); two of the former rare. 3 p

ITALY.

1988 PAPAL; Clement XIII., 1739; quarter-scudo.
1989 —— Gregory XVI., 1834; 30 Baiocchi; uncir. Scarce.
1990 —— Pius IX.; 1860; 20 Baiocchi, and 1 Lira. 2 p
1991 —— Superb lot copper coins; no duplicates. 8 p

Miscellaneous Silver Coins.

1992 SICILY; rare old coppers; 10 Grani, and 10, 8, 6, and 5 Tornesi; from 1798 to 1859. Very fine lot. 8 p
1993 SARDINIA; copper coins of Charles Emanuel, Victor Emanuel, etc. 6 p
1994 —— 50 Centesimi, and other small silver coins; some belonging to Sweden, etc. 12 p
1995 LOMBARDY; 5 Lire of the Provisional Government of 1848. Very fine.
1996 —— Copper (5 and 1 Centesimi); same; uncir. 2 p
1997 ECCLESIASTICAL coins; quarter-crown size. 3 p
1998 COPPER coins. 4 p

MISCELLANEOUS SILVER COINS.

1999 CLUMP Daler; struck during the 30 years' war; very thick. Rare. Size 14
2000 CROWN of Erfurt, to commemorate the death of Gustavus Adolphus, 1632; very fine and rare. Size 26
2001 —— of George I.; for Brunswick and Luneberg; wild man and tree; rev. arms of England.
2002 HAMBURG City; fine coins, average 25 cents. 3 p
2003 HUNGARY, Germany, etc.; coins of quarter-crown size; Leopold I., Maria Therese, etc. 4 p
2004 SIMILAR lot; larger size. 10 p
2005 MEDALETS and Jetons; extremely fine; average quarter-dollar in value. 7 p
2006 CONVENTION Dollar of Austria; Frankfort, 1848; uncirculated.
2007 THALER of Prussia; 1871. Fine.
2008 HELVETIA and Holland; 2 and 1 Franc. 2 p
2009 MISCELLANEOUS; int'c value, one-eighth dollar ea. 10 p
2010 —— With a few base. Fine lot. 43 p
2011 JEWISH Shekels; fine silver; two varieties. Very fine.

2012 MEDAL; battle of Rosbach; copper gilt.
2013 —— Siege of Breslau; copper. Rare.
2014 —— Similar, but with "defender of the Protestant Faith;" copper.
2015 MEDALS and Jetons. Good lot. 8 p

ADDENDA.

AMERICAN, COLONIAL, AND STATE COINS.

2016 TIN piece of James II.; Rosa, Americana, and Wood's pennies, and North American token; poor. 5 p
2017 NOVA Constellatio and Franklin Cents. 6 p
2018 NOVA Cæsarea; varieties; fair. 5 p
2019 AUCTORE Connec; unusual variety. 8 p
2020 VERMON Auctori; scarce; poor.
2021 COMMONWEALTH of Mass.; 1787 & 1788; good pair. 2 p
2022 —— Same; Half-cents, each year; very desirable. 2 p
2023 —— Same; Cents of 1788; ordinary. 2 p
2024 TALBOT, Allum & Lee cent; 1794. Very good.
2025 BAR pattern cent; no date. Very fine.

CENTS.

2026 1793; wreath; sharp impression, but cleaned. Rare.
2027 ——; Liberty cap; electrotyped.
2028 1794; a dark cent; little worn.
2029 1795; thick planchet; plain edge; dark. Fair.
2030 1796; Liberty cap behind head. *Fine*; rare.
2031 —— Head bound with a fillet, also very good.
2032 1797. Very good.
2033 1798. Ordinary.
2034 1799. Rather poor, but very rare.
2035 1800. Poor.
2036 1801. Very good. Dark.
2037 1802. Fine. Good color.
2038 1803. Fine.
2039 1804. Very fair; has two marks of a lathe drill on the head.
2040 1805. Fine for date. Scarce.
2041 —— Same with 1806. Both fine and scarce. 2 p
2042 1807. Two varieties. Fair. 2 p

Addenda.

2043 1808. Very fair for date. Scarce.
2044 1809. Equally fair, and more scarce.
2045 1810-11-12. All very fair.   3 p
2046 1813-14. Same.   2 p
2047 1816. Two varieties. Very fine.   2 p
2048 1817. With 13 and 15 stars. Good pair.   2 p
2049 1818-19-20. Fine.   3 p
2050 1821. Fine. Desirable.
2051 1822. Same generally, but with a scratch.
2052 1823. Good for date. Scarce.
2053 1824. Poor.
2054 1825. Fine.
2055 1826-27. Fine.   2 p
2056 1828-29-30. Ordinary.   3 p
2057 1831. Fine. Desirable.
2058 1832. Equally fine. Almost uncirculated.
2059 1833-34-35. Very fine.   3 p
2060 1836. Very fine (perfect die.)
2061 1837. Fine, but dark.
2062 1838. Uncirculated.
2063 1839. Three varieties; fine. Desirable.   3 p
2064 1840. Dark. Ordinary.
2065 1841-42. Both fine.   2 p
2065*1843-44. Ordinary.   2 p
2066 1845-46. Very good.
2067 1847. Uncirculated; red. Scarce.
2068 1848-49. Fine.   2 p
2069 1850 to '56 inclusive. Bright.   7 p
2070 1857. Fine.
2071 Nickel cents from 1857 to '75 inclusive.   20 p
2072 1868. Small proof sets, five and three cents nickel, and two and one cents, copper.
2073 1869. Same.
2074 1872. Same.
2075 1873. Same.
2076 1874. Same.
2077 1875. Same.
2078 Different dates. Five proofs, similar to last.

Addenda.

Half Cents.

2079	1794. Very good. Circulated.	
2080	1795. Thick and thin planchet. Very good.	2 p
2081	1797, 1800, and 1803. Ordinary.	3 p
2082	1804–5–6–9–10. All fine.	5 p
2083	1811. Good for date. Scarce.	
2084	1826–28. Rather ordinary.	2 p
2085	1828. Uncirculated.	
2086	1829–32–33–34. Fair lot.	4 p
2087	1835–37 (pure copper). Fine.	2 p
2088	1849 to '57 inclusive, without '52. Fine.	8 p
2089	Planchet for copper cent; two Feuchtwangers of '37. Washington double-head and speel-marke.	5 p

Dollars.

2090	1795. Flowing hair. Very fair.
2091	1797. Six stars before face. Fair.
2092	1798. Usual type. Fair.
2093	1799. Usual. Fine.
2094	1800. Very fair.
2095	1803. Ordinary.
2096	1842. Fine. Circulated.
2097	1847. Very fine. Scarce.
2098	1873. Nearly uncirculated. Scarce.
2099	1874. Trade dollar. Brilliant proof.

Half Dollars.

2100	1794. Fair for date.	
2101	1795. Same.	
2102	1803. Fine for date, but much circulated.	
2103	1805 over 1804. Very fine. Scarce.	
2104	1805–7. Fair.	2 p
2105	1808–9. Fair.	2 p
2106	1810. Very good.	
2107	1811–12. Both fine.	2 p
2108	1814–17. Both fine.	2 p
2109	1821. Very fine.	
2110	1822. Fine.	

Addenda. 113

2111 1823–24. Very fine.
2112 1825. Same.
2113 1826. Same.
2114 1827. Extremely fine.
2115 1828. Same.
2116 1829. Nearly proof. Beautiful.
2117 1831–34. Very fine.   2 p
2118 1835. Very fine.
2119 1837. Extremely fine. Scarce.
2120 1844–46. Very fine.   2 p
2121 1858. Very fine. Scarce.
2122 1862. Fine proof.
2123 1864. Fine proof.
2124 1865. Very fine.
2125 1867. Fine proof.
2126 1868. Extremely fine.
2127 1869. Extremely fine.

Quarter Dollars.

2128 1805. Fair for date. Scarce.
2129 1806. Better.
2130 1807. Ordinary.
2131 1818. Fine.
2132 1820. Fine.
2133 1822. Ordinary. Scarce.
2134 1825. Fine.
2135 1828. Fine.
2136 1831. Very fine.
2137 1834. Very fine.
2138 1835. Fine.
2139 1836. Fine.
2140 1837. Very fine.
2141 1838. Very fine. Varieties.   2 p
2142 1839–40. Very good.   2 p
2143 1845–46. Fine.   2 p
2144 1847. Extremely fine.
2145 1849–51. Fine.   2 p
2146 1853. Arrows removed.
2147 1860–62. Extremely fine.   2 p

8

2148 1863. Brilliant proof.
2149 1864–65–67. Extremely fine. 3 p
2150 1873–75. Extremely fine. 2 p
2151 1875. Plain edge; brilliant proof. Rare.

Dimes.

2152 1796. Ordinary, but scarce.
2153 1798. Very poor, but scarce.
2154 1801. Also very poor.
2155 1805. Fair for date. Scarce.
2156 1807. Poor. Scarce.
2157 1811–14. Both scarce. Very fair. 2 p
2158 1820–21. Both fine. 2 p
2159 1822. Poor. Scarce.
2160 1823–24. Ordinary. 2 p
2161 1825–27. Very fair. 2 p
2162 1829. Very fine.
2163 1830 and '31. Very fine. 2 p
2164 1832 and '33. Same. 2 p
2165 1835 and '37. Extremely fine. 2 p
2166 1837 and '38. Varieties; very fine. 3 p
2167 1839 and '40. Fine. 2 p
2168 1841 and '43. Fine. 2 p
2169 1844. Poor. Scarce.
2170 1845 and '46. Very fine and scarce. 2 p
2171 1847 and '49. " 2 p
2172 1850 and '51. " 2 p
2173 1853. Two varieties. 2 p
2174 1856. Two varieties. Ordinary. 2 p
2175 1857 and '59. Extremely fine. 2 p
2176 1860 and '62. Very fine. 2 p
2177 1863 and '64. Brilliant. Uncirculated. 2 p
2178 1865 and '72. Very fine. 2 p
2179 1873. With arrow-heads, and without. Very fine. 2 p
2180 1867, '69 and '70. Brilliant. 3 p

Half-Dimes.

2181 1795. Fair for date. Scarce.
2182 1800. Ordinary. Very scarce.

Addenda. 115

2183 1801. Poor. Very scarce.
2184 1829. Extremely fine.
2185 1831. Uncirculated. Brilliant.
2186 1832 and '33. Extremely fine. 2 p
2187 1834.   "   "
2188 1835. Two varieties. Fine. 2 p
2189 1836. Very fine.
2190 1837. Two varieties. Extremely fine. 2 p
2191 1838, '39 and '40. Very fine. 3 p
2192 1844. Ordinary. Scarce.
2193 1853, '54, '56, '57, '58, and '60. Very fine. 6 p
2194 1862, '63, '64, '65, and '67. Brilliant. 5 p
2194* 1868, '69, '70, '72, and '73. Very fine. 5 p

Three Cents.

2195 1851, '52, '55, '56, '59, '60, '61, '63, '65, '70, and '73. All fine, and several proofs. 11 p

Electrotypes.

2196 Dollar of 1836. Well made.
2197 Cent of 1791; Washington and large eagle.
2198 Cent of 1792; from half-dollar die. Very fine.
2199 Franco-Americana, and others. 3 p

American Medals and Tokens.

2200 Gen. Lafayette; rev. The defender, etc.; bronze proof.
2201 Stonewall Jackson; tin.
2202 Washington Tokens; (Unity States, and Abraham's card.) 2 p
2203 Anti-slavery, etc.; tokens and Melanotypes. 6 p
2204 Prince of Wales; visit, etc. Extra fine. 4 p
2205 Postage Stamps; in brass mountings; Melanotypes, etc. 6 p
2206 Sutler's Token; J. Benson; good for 50 cents, etc. 4 p
2207 Great Eastern, Bolen, Pioneer base ball club, and Bunker Hill Centennial. 4 p
2208 McClellan; rev. Washington and National Peace Jubilee, Boston, 1869. 2 p

116   *Addenda.*

2210 Lexington Centennial; in brass and tin.   2 p
2211 Col. James Fisk; " Relief for Chicago." Rare.
2212 Shinplasters and cards. Fine.   13 p
2213 Same, in brass; Jackson; rev. mule. Rare.
2214 Louis Kossuth; 3 varieties. Fine.   3 p
2215 Jackson and Clay; brass tokens. Very fine.   2 p
2216 Scott, Fremont, and Pierce.   "   3 p
2217 Fremont, Scott, and Harrison.   "   4 p
2218 Clay, Harrison, and Johnson.   3 p
2219 Political Copperheads, with busts; and large copper-
     heads with cards.   31 p

Foreign Silver Coins.

2220 James I. (England); Irish sixpence and English shilling,
     etc. Poor, scarce.   3 p
2221 George II. and III. and Victoria; shilling, 2 sixpences,
     and threepence.   4 p
2222 George III.; shilling, 1787; beautiful uncirculated
     example, with no dot above the head of the King.
     Very rare.
2223 Dollar of Mexico, 1770. Pierced.
2224 Half-dollar of same, while an *Empire* in 1866; Maxi-
     milian, Emperor. Rare.
2225 Same of Bolivia; with bust of Bolivar. Base.
2226 Louis XVI., King of France, 1791; 30 and 15 sols.
                                                      2 p
2227 Sierra Leone; 10 cents; Lion; good and rare; with
     miscellaneous of av. value.   15 p
2228 Base Coins.   11 p

Copper Medals, Coins, and Tokens.

2229 William Shakespeare; bust; rev. plain.   Size 32
2230 Voltaire; bust; rev. plain. Extra fine.   "   22
2231 Henry IV. and Louis XVIII.; rev. inscription. " 22
2232 Louis XIV.; The King of Prussia (Fred. the Great);
     and 3 tin medals.   5 p
2233 Heavy Coins of 5 copecs, and 10 granis, and 10 fornesi
     value; Russian and Sicilian.   5 p

Addenda.

2234 LARGE Coins of France; 10 centimes, 5 sols, etc. Good lot. 6 p
2235 ENGLISH and English Colonial pennies. 14 p
2236 LARGE Portugese pennies. 8 p
2237 SAME of Uruguay, Buenos Ayres, etc. 10 p
2238 TEMPO (Japan); cash, etc. 8 p
2239 HALF-PENNY size; selected; very fine; altogether unclassified and miscellaneous. 10 p
2240 SAME; Canadian. Good lot. 20 p
2241 SAME; English. 12 p
2242 SAME; French and German. 12 p
2243 FARTHING size; mixed. 14 p
2244 —— Same; Charles II. England. Rare and fine.
2245 MISCELLANEOUS coppers. 31 p
2246 TOKENS of Napoleon I., Prince Albert and Napoleon III. Very fine. 4 p
2247 NAPOLEON on an Ass with the Devil for company; with pattern or model guineas, etc. 9 p
2248 CHINESE Junk token, and two French. Fine. 3 p
2249 SHEKELS, in copper and tin, not in the ancient style, but very fine. 2 p

2250 ANCIENT Coins of Augustus and Trajan; second size fine. 2 p
2251 —— Gordianus Africanus I.; rev. female seated holding sceptre, SECVRITAS (see Wellenheim 12,771, where it is marked R 4); better than a merely fair example of this rare coin. G. B.
2252 FAUSTINA and a Gothic; first size. 2 p
2253 FALSE Medallion of Nero. Fine.
2254 ROMAN and Greek. A pretty lot. 11 p

2255 HALF-DOLLARS (United States); 1803 and 1811. Ordinary. 2 p
2256 —— 1814 and 1823. 2 p
2257 —— 1824 and 1827. Extremely fine. 2 p

2258 QUARTER-DOLLARS, 1805. Ordinary. 2 p
2259 —— 1807 and 1818. The last fine. 2 p
2260 —— 1822 and 1825. Fine. 2 p
2261 —— 1836 and 1837. Very fine. 2 p
2262 —— 1838. " 2 p
2263 —— 1838 and 1839. " 2 p
2264 —— 1839 and 1840. " 2 p
2265 —— 1845 and 1846. " 2 p
2266 —— 1847 and 1849. " 2 p
2267 —— 1862 and 1873. One fine proof. 2 p
2268 DIMES, 1796 and 1814. Ordinary, rare. 2 p
2269 —— 1820 and 1821. Fine for date. 2 p
2270 —— 1837. Two varieties; very fine. 2 p
2271 —— 1838 and 1841. Fine. 2 p
2272 —— 1843 and 1845. Very fine. 2 p
2273 —— 1850 and 1851. 2 p
2274 —— 1853 and 1859. Extremely fine. 2 p
2275 —— 1860 and 1863. " 2 p
2276 —— 1869 and 1873. " 2 p
2277 HALF-DIMES, 1795. Ordinary. 2 p
2278 —— 1800. Ordinary; scarce.
2279 —— 1829, 1831, 1833 (2). Extra fine. 4 p
2280 —— 1834, 1835, 1837 (2). Fine. 4 p
2281 —— 1838, 1840, 1844. 4 p
2282 —— 1844, 1849, and 50 others. (All fine.) 7 p
2283 PROF. 5, 3, and 1 cent, 1875. 3 p
2284 SAME, repeated. 3 p
2285 —— Same. 3 p
2286 CENT, 1797 and 1798. Ordinary. 2 p
2287 —— 1802. Very good; scarce.
2288 —— 1817 and 1836. Fair and fine. 2 p
2289 —— From 1848, with duplicates to 1856. Bright and uncirculated. 12 p
2290 SUCCESS to the United States; token in brass. Large size, fine.
2291 DUPLICATE; with Mott's token. 2 p
2292 NOVA-CONSTELLATIO; two varieties. Fair. 2 p
2293 MASSACHUSETTS half-cent, 1788. Very fine, rare.
2294 NICKEL cents, 1857 and '58. Uncirculated. 2 p

Numismatic Books. 119

2295 SHINPLASTERS of 1837 and '41. Uncirculated. 3 p
2296 SIMON ROLFE in Sarum; his half-penny, 1660; farthing size. Good, and very rare.
2297 EMMANUEL DE ROHAN, Grand Master of the Knights of Malta; a half-dollar, or 15 Tari piece of 1796. Very fine and rare.
2298 NAPOLEON I.; two francs of 1806, by *Tiolier*. Fair.
2299 QUARTER Tical of Siam (15 cents); elephant; rev. three pavillions, with half of same. Fine and rare. 2 p
2300 DANISH and Italian; small silver. 4 p

NUMISMATIC BOOKS.

2301 ACKERMAN's Ancient Coins, with illustrations; cloth bound, octavo. London, 1846
2302 ——— Roman coins, with numerous plates; 2 vols., cloth, oct. London, 1834
2303 ——— Introduction to Ancient and Modern Coins; 12mo., London, 1848
2304 ——— Coins of the Romans, with illustrations; cloth, oct. London, 1844
2305 RUDING's Annals of the Coinage of Great Britain, 1 vol., plates; cloth, quarto, 3 vols. London, 1840
2306 MADDEN's Jewish Coinage, with 250 wood-cuts, rough edges, top gilt, oct. London, 1864
2307 PINKERTON's Medallic History of England, with 40 fine plates; cloth, quarto. London, 1802
2308 SIMON's Essay on Irish Coins, with Snelling's supplement; numerous plates, quarto. Dublin, 1810
2309 EDE's Complete View of the Gold and Silver Coins of all Nations; 34 pages of illustrations; small quarto. London, 1808
2310 SNELLING's Current Coins of Europe, with 25 copper-plates; 12mo. London, 1765
2311 HUMPHREY's Coinage of the British Empire, with illustrations; cloth, quarto; binding loose. London, 1854
2312 CONDER's Coins, Tokens, and Medalets of Great Britain, Ireland, and Colonies; post oct. Ipswich, 1798

120   *Addenda.*

2313 MOORISH MONEY. A History by Ignatius Pietraszew-
ski; half morocco; quarto, with numerous illustrations.   Berlin, 1843

2314 MILLAN's Coins, Weights, and Measures of all Nations;
old calf, 12mo.   1747

2315 CARDWELL's Lectures on the Coinage of the Greeks and
Romans; cloth, oct.   Oxford, 1832

2316 AUGUSTINI (Antoni). Familæ Romanæ; full of plates,
calf; folio.   Rome, 1577

2317 —— Another, by same; same title, but a different
work; a translation by *Sada*; folio, vellum.
  Rome, 1650

2318 ADRIANI Relandi. Dissertationes Quatuor de Nummis,
etc.; with many illustrations; vellum, 12mo.
  Rhenum, 1706

2319 VAILLANT's Numismata Imperatorum Romanorum; old
calf, quarto; fully illustrated.   Paris, 1694

2320 —— Same title; vellum, 3 vols., folio.   Rome, 1743
  [Beautiful copy.]

2321 SESTINI Museo Hedervariani, with splendid illustrations;
vellum, 2 vols., quarto.   Firenze, 1829

2322 OMNIBONI Comment In Ciceronem; half calf; small
folio.   Venet, 1476

2323 LITES Grave Del Museo Kircheriano; half morocco,
folio; fully illustrated.   Rome, 1839

2324 PATIN's Familiæ Romanæ; illustrated, half calf, folio.
  Paris, 1673

2325 FELT's Massachusetts Currency, etc., illustrated.
Quarto, cloth.   Boston, 1839

2326 AMERICAN Journal of Numismatics; first, second, third,
and fourth vols.; half morocco, in two vols.; *Very
rare.*   N. Y., 1866–70

ENGLISH CATALOGUES.

[All bound.]

2327 1830. Collection of James, Earl of Morton; Greek
and Roman Coins; 737 lots, priced and named.

2328 1831. Anglo-Gallic coins, with addena of gems; 507
lots, priced and named.

Numismatic Books. 121

2329 1832. Marmaduke Trattle; 3,387 lots, priced and named.
2330 1837. Robert Surtees and another (together), both priced and named.
2331 1841. Sir John Twisden, Dymock, Sir Robert Abdy, and Matthew Young; partly priced and named.
2332 1842. Various catalogues; Eq. Rev. G. F. Nott; British Museum; Dean of St. Patrick, etc.; bound together.
2333 1842. Rev. G. F. Nott's Catalogue alone; 1,375 lots, neatly priced and named.
2334 1846. Cavalier Campana, Rome; neatly priced and named; 1,706 lots.
2335 1848. Twenty-four Catalogues, together; partly priced.
2336 1850. Twelve Catalogues; together.
2337 1852. H. L. Tovey; priced and named, 663 lots.
2338 BUNDLE of English Catalogues; paper covers. 12 p
2339 BUNDLE sale; mostly Lincoln & Sons; the lot.
2340 NORTON's Literary Letter; W. E. Woodward's Tenth Sale, priced and named; Akerman's List of Wiltshire Tokens, etc., with a number of curious manuscripts in one lot. 14 p
2341 MASON's Monthly Coin and Stamp Magazine for 1870, with other matter; the lot.

PRICED CATALOGUES.

2342 1859. J. N. T. Levick's Collection; large paper copy. Philadelphia
2343 1865. W. E. W.'s 6th sale.
2344 1870. Leonard & Co. Boston
2345 1870. Leavitt, Strebeigh & Co., April 28-9.
2346 1870. Fewsmith Cabinet.
2347 1871. Bangs, Merwin & Co.; Canada Collection.
2348 1871. Elliott Collection; G. A. L. & Co.
2349 1871. L. Strebeigh & Co.
2350 1872. Bangs, Merwin & Co.
2351 1872. Charles Furman and others.

2352 1872. Thos. Birch & Son; C. N. Body's Collection.
2353 1873. I. F. Wood's Collection.
2354 1873. Chubbuck Collection.
2355 1873. H. C. Bird & Co., Auct'rs.
2356 1874. W. E. W.'s 18th sale.
2357 1874. Coins and bric-a-brac.
2358 1874. Groux Collection.
2359 1874. H. Sandford's Collection.
2360 1874. Edward Cogan's Sale.
2361 1875. John W. Haseltine's Sale.   N. Y.
2362 1875. —— Same.   Philadelphia
2363 1875. Joseph E. Gay's Sale.
2364 1875. Edward Cogan's Sale.
2365 1875. Stenz Collection.
2366 1875. Haseltine's Sale.   Philadelphia
2367 1874. —— Same.
2368 1875. E. Cogan's Sale.
2369 Bundle (24) Catalogues.
2370 —— Same; with Brown's Curiosity Cabinet.   26 p
2372 Lot of old newspapers, parchments, manuscripts, and Confederate money.

2373 Victoria rupee and George III. half-crown.   2 p
2374 Itzbu, Japan; and cut silver plug, used as a coin.   2 p
2375 Half-rupee and English shilling.   2 p
2376 Coin, with a mixture of gold, size of English half-groat, and other coins of silver, French, Spanish, etc.; dime size.   6 p
2377 Dime, and dime size.   4 p
2378 Half-dime, and same size.   4 p
2379 Small silver coins.   11 p
2380 Half-cent of 1793; very fair for date, and rare.
2381 Cent of 1820; uncirculated.
2382 —— of 1794 (die of '93), Franklin cent, and 1817, 15 stars.   3 p
2383 —— of 1805, '12, '27, '30, and '39.   5 p
2384 —— of 1856; nickel. Fine, rare.

www.ingramcontent.com/pod-product-compliance
Lightning Source LLC
Chambersburg PA
CBHW031345160426
43196CB00007B/736